A Journey Into the Heart of Matter

by

Sue Martin DF Astrol S

Grosvenor House
Publishing Limited

This book is published by
Grosvenor House Publishing Ltd
28-30 High Street, Guildford, Surrey, GU1 3HY.
www.grosvenorhousepublishing.co.uk

A CIP record for this book
is available from the British Library

ISBN 978-1-907211-67-6

Foreword

At the age of twelve, sitting in an orchard, I asked "Who Am I" - suddenly, I found I was outside of my body, looking down onto my body - I thought "How useful my body is, how wonderful it is - but it is not me".

This altered state of awareness occurred naturally, I had not been trying to meditate, or to raise my consciousness - at the age of twelve, I had no conception of meditation, higher consciousness, or altered states of awareness.

My lasting impression of that moment, was of being in an energetic field of such grace and peace - and in that "holding field" a key of remembrance dropped into my consciousness.

This was the start of my journey.

Contents

Introduction

"When you were young and your heart was an open book. You used to say, live and let live...
But in this ever changing world in which we live in....."

Paul Mᶜ Cartney *Musician*

Indeed, it is an ever changing world that we live in, and for all of us, this lack of solidity and pace of change, has been exhilarating, breathtaking and even, for astrologers who have a map, downright disorientating!

Our science, our craft, our love, goes back into the mists of time. We have been proud of the fact that we understand a language that has spanned many thousands of years and that our connection to the Cosmos unites cultures, races and creeds through this unfolding Universal language.

Our language was safe, solid and based on data that stood the test of time. For centuries life has continued within a fairly defined spectrum, but over the last two hundred or so years this has radically changed.

Now the speed of change has gone into another gear with the arrival of Asteroids, Centaurs, Kuiper Belt objects, Dwarf Planets etc., our map of the Universe is being constantly up dated, shape shifted and downloaded with more and more information.

So how are we, as astrologers, to understand and integrate the expansion of awareness that is being unfolded through the recent discoveries in outer space?

In order to assimilate and comprehend the expansion of information which is flooding into our awareness, I believe that astrological knowledge needs to unite with

3

the teachings of ancient wisdom and quantum physics – for although each are speaking a different language, each is pointing to a fundamental truth and each discipline is leading us to a wholeness far greater than its separate parts.

It is time to step out of our astrological comfort zone and take stock of where we are now – to redefine the purpose of astrology as we journey through the first decade of the 21st Century.

We need to see how astrology links and interpenetrates other disciplines and how, combining the knowledge contained within these other fields, we create a far deeper understanding of what it is to be a human being on Planet Earth.

If we take these steps, then astrology can unite and, indeed, expand the growth of awareness that is flooding into the Earth plane.

This book is not intended to be an astrological reference book, but comes from a desire to bring together and synthesize current knowledge with ancient wisdom through the eyes of an astrologer.

As such it is a guide, and a stepping stone into this vaster arena.

As astrologers, we are working with a large canvas and this book has been painted in large brush strokes.

Each chapter within this book covers a particular theme, but all of the chapters are interrelated and, rather like a jigsaw puzzle, it is not until the last piece is put into place that the whole picture comes to life.

So I would ask you to read this book with an open mind and heart and allow the jigsaw to take shape.

This book has been written to give language and form to the astrology, or cosmo-biology that is being revealed at this point in time.

It has also been written to highlight the vast potential that awaits us all and to show how, in the 21st Century, cosmo-biology can benefit and encourage a far deeper understanding and appreciation of the infinite beauty, interconnectedness and sacredness of all Life, as we grow beyond our present day belief patterns.

March 2009

Chapter 1

Evolving Through Time and Space

"We are the local embodiment of the Cosmos grown to self-awareness. We have begun to contemplate our origins; star stuff pondering the stars."

Carl Sagan *Philosopher*

As you read this you are travelling through space at some 65,000 miles an hour, journeying around our local star, the Sun, taking approximately 365 days to complete one year – a Solar return.

The Sun, in turn, orbits the Galaxy. Our Galaxy is said to be composed of some 500 billion stars and is so huge that the Sun requires some 230 million Earth years, or so, to complete one orbit around the Milky Way's centre – marking out a Cosmic Year.

The Milky Way too, in its turn, is orbiting around a point in space called the Super Galactic Centre that we circle and spiral through. An infinite field - worlds within worlds.

The distances are vast and yet, from within the depth of the smallest particle forming each individual cell out to the furthest points of the Galaxy and beyond, everything is intricately and exquisitely interconnected within a matrix of electro magnetic circuitry.

Every element on Earth, except for the lightest, was created in the heart of a massive star.

Lead and uranium were produced in a supernova explosion during the cataclysmic end of a huge star's life. According to physicists, these elements were ejected into space by the force of the massive explosion, where they mixed with other matter and formed new stars and planets.

And so it is that aeons of years ago the stardust from exploding stars became part of the miracle of the origin of life on Earth

That's why the Earth is so rich in these heavy elements. The iron in our blood and the calcium in our bones were all forged in such stars and we are the physical manifestation of this starlight.

Quantum physicists talk of a holographic or morphogenetic field underlying and connecting physical matter.

Mystics talk of a vital force, Chi, Prana, or Shakti flowing in a pure field of Divine Consciousness in which all is manifested and created.

Both speak of a subtle field that interpenetrates and enfolds all atomic structure on Planet Earth.

It is true, that in our daily, earthly lives our experience is of physical form, however, on a subtle level, everything, from a blade of grass to the most distant star, is energy at different states of vibration and resonance and we are, in fact, part of this one Universal energetic Field.

From the moment that we embody our physical form we are, and are in, an energetic exchange of light and particle and each of the cycles of each of the planetary bodies informs and develops this subtle energetic system.

There is a timeless journey unfolding through each of our lives, from the first breath, when we connect into the Earth's energy and the Light of the stellar Sun, through the cycles of the Moon, Mercury, Venus, Mars, out through the Asteroid Belt, to Jupiter, Saturn, via Chiron to Uranus, Neptune, Pluto and beyond, we are encoding our reception and response to the subtle planetary resonances and harmonics as they orbit through the holographic, stellar, quantum field.

Quantum mechanics and cellular biology are at the cutting edge of reuniting Mind, Body and Spirit and equally, our innate interconnection with the Universal energy field via the Cosmos.

To quote Bruce Lipton, a leading cellular biologist and author of 'The Biology of Belief: Unleashing the Power of Consciousness, Matter and Miracles'

"A century ago a group of creative minorities launched a radical new view of how the Universe works. Albert Einstein, Max Planck and Werner Heisenberg, among others, formulated new theories concerning the underlying mechanics of the Universe.

Their work on quantum mechanics revealed that the Universe is not an assembly of physical parts as suggested by Newtonian physics but is derived from a holistic entanglement of immaterial energy waves.

11

Quantum mechanics shockingly reveals that there is no true 'physicality' in the Universe; atoms are made of focussed vortices of energy – miniature tornados that are constantly popping into and out of existence.

Atoms as energy fields interact with the full spectrum of invisible energy fields that comprise the Universe intimately entangled with one another and the field in which they are immersed.

This new perspective of human biology does not view the body as just a mechanical device, but rather incorporates the role of a mind and spirit."

The suggestion that there is no true physicality and, that underpinning our atomic structure, mind and spirit is informing the cellular system, is so profound and transformative to the Saturnian mind that when it is finally recognised by humanity as a whole, the shockwaves will create a radical quantum shift.

A shift that is so life changing that our earlier errors in believing that the Earth was flat and central to the Solar system, will pale into insignificance.

So as humans, we need to recognise, accept and embrace the realisation that we are primarily energetic beings linking into a conscious holographic field and far more than just a physical form.

If we take on board the findings of Max Planck, Einstein and others then it is not a great leap of faith to understand that astrology is the study of how sub-atomic particles of light in matter, imprint and inform cellular structure and indeed the whole of our third dimensional physical reality.

What is so beautiful is that astrology reveals the interface between this quantum soup of 'invisible energy fields' as they interact upon each individual's sub-atomic energy field hidden within the cellular atomic whole.

Or put another way, astrology, or cosmo-biology, is the print out for any given moment in time of the state of resonance, vibration and consciousness of an individual, or group of individuals and indeed of all Life Forms.

And, just like the ever flowing, fluctuating Cosmos, the study of astrology is not contained or held within a static circle.

When we look at an astrological chart we are, in fact, looking at a two dimensional flat depiction of a multi-dimensional experience, for the astrological chart mirrors a moment in time in a flowing, spinning, whirlwind of particle, wave, light, energy and motion.

The term 'Jyotish' from Vedic astrology means exactly that - the 'Science of Light' or the 'Light of God'.

Language, which is such a gift, can equally divide, separate and splinter. Words have such an effect upon our unconscious belief patterns.

Certain words can bring up some resistance – as a generality, anyone with a more mystical/Neptunian emphasis will probably be more comfortable with the words 'Light of God' and the scientific/Uranian community may prefer the phrase 'Science of Light'.

Equally, the name of God is interchangeable with Allah, Jehovah, Source, Universal Consciousness, Being, Goddess, All That Is .....

Whatever our individual beliefs are, we need to look for the common root that we all share as humanity on Planet Earth, which underpins all of our thought processes for as Martin Luther King said, "We either come together as brothers, or perish together as fools" This is the strength of our astrological language for at its root astrology has no gender, racial or religious bias – planetary movement and resonance does not care if you are Jew, Arab, black, white, male or female – energy in itself is a pure source. As such it spans the spectrum of humanity in a unifying focus.

Knowing that we all have our origins in the same stardust too and that we are one Global family, spiralling through time and space, might be a good start to recognising our innate interconnectedness.

Encouragingly, the recent discoveries made within the scientific community have the potential to also bring about a cohesion that unifies all creeds and races, for as more and more is being revealed within the quantum field, scientific discovery is unifying and linking with the tenets of ancient wisdom.

The creed of separation and a mechanical Universe is a modern belief of the Newtonian period and one that is being rapidly amended by recent discoveries.

As astrologers we know that astrological cycles are not random. Within this enfolding cosmic dance there is a pattern and a pathway, which we, as human beings, intimately link with on our evolutionary journey.

At some level, as astrologers, we have always understood our interconnection with the Cosmos. Indeed we are the Community that has held the unifying principle of 'As Above – So Below' at the very heart of our study. But are we truly aware that, en masse, mankind is interconnecting with the planetary cycles flowing through a 'quantum soup' and that whilst we are embodied we are permanently translating these subtle pulses of light, wave and particle into physical manifestation through our cellular body as physical development/degeneration, emotional/mental reaction and potential spiritual growth.

It now appears that the scientific community are about to link with the mystical community in giving a scientific explanation to what astrologers have witnessed and owned for centuries.

Marianne Williamson describes this renaissance of understanding as being 'A collective knowing that a dimension of reality exists beyond the material plane and that sense of knowing is causing a mystical resurgence on the planet today. It's not just children who are looking for a missing piece. It is a very mature outlook to question the nature of our reality.'

Chapter 2

A Moment in Time

*'Every situation, every moment - is of infinite worth;
for it is the representative of a whole eternity.'*

Goethe *Writer*

All moments in time are precious, but there are some moments in time that are also pivotal.

Our group evolution is accelerated and marked out by specific planetary alignments and discoveries.

They are "Markers in Time" – a moment when the group consciousness says "We are ready for the next evolutionary curve – the next awakening!"

As we approach the culmination of this Piscean Age we are stepping into new territory. This particular marker in time is marking the completion of a cycle that began some 5000 years ago which, in turn, is linking into a cycle that began around two hundred million years ago.

Here on Earth, for aeons of time, Saturn has been the conscious outer boundary, the container, or gestational sac that has held Life on Earth.

As human beings we lived with this perception, developing the material world, becoming adept within the physical laws of this reality.

But then this sac was breached in 1781 by the discovery of Uranus, in 1846 by Neptune and by Pluto in 1930.

Over the last 250 years, Uranus, Neptune and Pluto have been pulsing, dissolving and penetrating this sac with the aim to fundamentally expand our awareness and potential beyond our inherited, saturnine belief patterns focussed on a purely 3rd dimensional reality.

Now our cosmic reference points seem to change by the year.

If the maxim 'As Above, So Below' is still correct and there is no reason to doubt it, then it would appear that we, as human beings, at this moment in time, in witnessing the rapid expansion of our cosmic theatre, are equally rapidly expanding, and morphing into a monumental growth of consciousness.

To bring this into balance, we have to recognise that, the often forgotten, 'As Within – So Without' is also a fundamental and intrinsic part of the equation. For 'As Above – So Below' can only outwardly reflect what is contained within. 'As Within – So Without' is the rudder, or the focal point which allows access to the subtle fields and from this interaction, our inner, individual states of consciousness have a profound effect upon the cosmic loom and outer appearances.

Each individual's experience of planetary aspects and transits reflect their unique awareness, consciousness and inner potential, revealing the harmony, balance and interplay, or otherwise, between the inner and outer Universes.

Planetary aspects and transits unfold in a multitude of ways and in ways that have yet to be seen. The core essence and resonance of the planets, signs and houses underpin the pattern, but the revelation of these planetary dynamics is person specific.

For centuries we have lived in a Society that has been filled with information and guidelines where we have been educated along narrow paths within a pre-defined spectrum and this too could equally be said for the study of astrology.

Certain aspects, signs and planets have been deemed to fall into a particular category. Is this an absolute - a reality – or is it a group unconscious response to behavioural patterns and reactions that have been built up, and stored over large cycles of time, that have formed a sub-script in our own unconsciousness that we individually experience once again at a Saturn return, or a Pluto square?

Nothing is written in stone and as we journey through these next decades we will come to recognise that our individual state of consciousness, our thoughts and feelings have a profound effect upon how planetary cycles unfold. Our individual and group 'influence' will become markedly more pronounced, for we are entering a time of major transformation and uncharted potential.

Now is the time to take another look at our belief structure, to see where we may be just repeating past patterns of engrained experience and interpretation rather than assisting in an evolutionary journey of discovery.

This evolutionary journey of discovery is alive and present in every breath and heart beat.

Today, many astrologers see astrology as simply a symbolic language, rather than a metaphysical reality that is operating through each of us moment by moment.

It is true, that we certainly work with the symbology of the planets, but each of these symbols is addressing a far greater metaphysical truth, for each of the planetary glyphs describes and takes us on an evolutionary journey in and through physical matter.

Each planet's symbol represents a compilation and synthesis of fundamental states of consciousness, resonance and existence which is seeking to manifest.

We illustrate and describe the Cross of Matter, the Half Circle of Soul and the Circle of Spirit each time we draw a planetary glyph and consciously, or unconsciously, we will open to these states of consciousness as we interpret a chart.

The Cross of Matter is the densest vibration. The Half Circle of Soul links to the emotional mental state of higher resonance and the Circle of Spirit takes us into the highest vibrational rates. Each interpenetrates the other, eternally creating and informing the physical and metaphysical worlds.

Once, as astrologers, we would have worked within the mystical and scientific community of the time. These concepts would have been part and parcel of astrological awareness.

The astrological symbol for the Sun, the 'Dot' within the 'Circle', was used by the ancient Egyptians to depict Ra, the Sun God. It is also the symbol for 'Bindu' the symbol used in Hindu scripture. 'The seed or source of Creation', 'The first particle of Transcendent Light'.

Para Bindu or Bindu is the subtle energy that underpins all matter, which modern day quantum physicists speak of and of which ancient mystics taught. Modern day scientists say that the whole Universe, just before coming into materialisation, would fit on the head of a pin creating a phenomenal point of energy – this point of energy or 'dot' equally describes Para Bindu.

So as astrologers, whether we are aware of it or not, we are describing concepts far larger, and far more inclusive, than a single individual when we work with the symbol for the Sun. We are working with the creative light force that flows throughout the Universe and equally within the tiniest particle of a single cell that is interlinked through time and space within the quantum field.

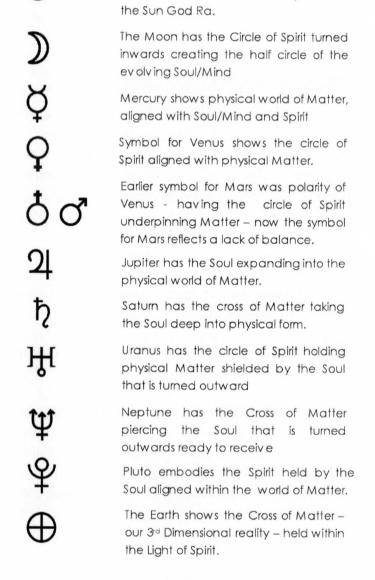

Pure Light of Source. Pure potential held within the Circle of Spirit. Light held within individual cells. Para Bindu. Symbol for the Sun God Ra.

The Moon has the Circle of Spirit turned inwards creating the half circle of the evolving Soul/Mind

Mercury shows physical world of Matter, aligned with Soul/Mind and Spirit

Symbol for Venus shows the circle of Spirit aligned with physical Matter.

Earlier symbol for Mars was polarity of Venus - having the circle of Spirit underpinning Matter – now the symbol for Mars reflects a lack of balance.

Jupiter has the Soul expanding into the physical world of Matter.

Saturn has the cross of Matter taking the Soul deep into physical form.

Uranus has the circle of Spirit holding physical Matter shielded by the Soul that is turned outward

Neptune has the Cross of Matter piercing the Soul that is turned outwards ready to receive

Pluto embodies the Spirit held by the Soul aligned within the world of Matter.

The Earth shows the Cross of Matter – our 3rd Dimensional reality – held within the Light of Spirit.

24

Contained within our astrological symbols is a language which unites both mysticism and quantum physics

Our metaphysical journey through the Cosmos is magnificent, mysterious and indeed quite mind blowing and it is during times of upheaval and change that we have the opportunity to break free from past limitations.

So let us explore our human potential with an expansive openness. To do this, we have first of all to awaken to the potential of what is possible beyond our current beliefs and expectations.

Or as Shakespeare said, so many moons ago "There are more things, Horatio, in Heaven and Earth, than are dreamt of in your philosophy!"

Chapter 3

Reflection

'Physicists do not need mysticism, and mystics do not need physics, but humanity needs both.'

Fritjof Capra *Physicist and Writer*

From a mystical perspective, there is a well trodden metaphysical pathway that we are passing through each lifetime. We incarnate through numerous lifetimes, flowing in a subtle energetic field that is alive with consciousness.

Many spiritual disciplines speak of this pathway – the Vedic Scriptures, the Qabalah, the teachings of the Sufis, Buddhists, Zoroastrians, Kahunas and the Gnostics all understood and indeed understand the journey of the human being on the path to enlightenment.

They speak of the indestructibility of the Spirit.

Ancient wisdom states that when we leave this physical life, our bodies (atomic structure) die, but the Essence, the Consciousness, the Soul, the light, subatomic, energetic structure, which interpenetrates the physical form lives on.

Mystics believe that at the point of our death we leave the physical realm to re-emerge within a quantum field of finer resonance, within a light body, which we inhabit until we reincarnate once more into physicality. We simply merge in and out of physical form, all the while transmuting denser forms of consciousness and energy into finer structure and resonance.

Mystical tradition states that our energetic Essence, or Soul, houses the sum total of all of our experiences throughout our journeys into physicality and that when we incarnate we are an aspect of this journey.

Energy and its properties have been explored and extensively described by the scientific community over many years.

It was Albert Einstein who proved that energy can be neither created nor destroyed, but only altered in form - reflecting and sharing the mystic's belief but spoken in another language.

During this decade the CERN experiment in Geneva known as the Large Hadron Collider, a huge particle accelerator, has as part of its remit, the investigation of the holographic field and other inter-dimensional fields.

In particular they are looking for the Higgs-Bosen particle, said to be the subatomic particle that underpins the matrix upon which physical form is built. The same 'Bindu' particle which the Vedic scriptures wrote of some 5000 years ago.

It seems that the more scientists explore and discover, the more mystery is revealed. However, it is during this particular age of quantum science, that more and more scientists are turning to an understating of how science and mysticism are reflecting each other.

So what does this mean for astrology? I believe we, as a community, understand the practical manifestation of these two other bodies of knowledge. Astrology is the fusion of both quantum physics and mysticism. For we watch the unfolding of this subtle, vital, electro magnetic energy or consciousness through time.

As astrologers we are very good at observation, noting what occurs when planets make certain aspects. We have been correlating this information for centuries.

We have become adept at the likely 'when' and 'what' surrounding an event and are past Masters at seeing the underlying planetary patterns that are involved in outer events.

For example we understand that this coming together of scientists and mystics is a reflection of the mutual reception of Uranus in Pisces and Neptune in Aquarius in which there is a natural potential to blend science and mysticism.

This merging began in earnest in 1993 when Uranus and Neptune commenced a new cycle making triple conjunctions on February 2nd, August 19th and October 24th, around 18 to 19 degrees of Capricorn.

As astrologers we would naturally see this as one of the potentials that might manifest during this planetary cycle – a cycle which culminates in 2165.

However, what we are not so good at seeing, or asking is 'How' and 'Why'?

These answers are to be found within the study of quantum physics and the wisdom of spiritual tradition.

It is as if we each hold a piece of the puzzle but until we integrate our respective knowledge we are missing the point of our radiant ride around the Sun.

As astrologers we recognise that at our birth we inherit a particular blend of planetary patterning and potential which is an image of a moment in time and a reflection of our core being - a core being that far transcends personality - for it is an aspect of energy, resonance, consciousness that is eternally flowing and evolving throughout the Cosmos.

As astrologers, our particular piece of the puzzle is the knowledge of how planets mark out time and evolution through the quantum field that scientists explore and equally, how our evolutionary growth, via these planetary cycles, refines our unique energetic fingerprint into higher and finer states of consciousness that mystics call the Soul.

Unfortunately, it does seem as if we have unconsciously put on dark glasses to hide ourselves from the Light that we are and, rather like a record on an old gramophone, we have been going around and around playing the same tune, repeating the song that has been passed down to us from generation to generation, held in a group consciousness that says

"This is how it is".

But all this is about to change, for as Pluto transits through Capricorn during these next several years, we have the opportunity to radically transform rigid belief patterns, fears and outdated limitations.

Many changes are likely, but In particular, we may uproot our understanding around death and truly come to know what mystics have always said and scientists are beginning to explain, that we are an energetic/ spiritual Being whose essence/soul cannot die.

We need to recognise that our current understanding of what it is to be a human being has been handed down to us. We are in effect the product of an overlay of information that has been passed down to us from generation to generation and as such is rarely questioned.

In truth we reflect and embody the information we are given and much of what we are given is an intellectual exercise, that labels life.

A young child may look up to the sky and see a form moving through the air, diving and darting in and out of clouds and ask 'What is that?' and be told 'A bird'.

This labelling and the naming of the form, satisfies the mind's curiosity and it is quietly filed away, until the next time this particular form appears.

One dictionary definition of a bird is ' A warm blooded, egg laying, feathered vertebrate'.

In the same way, one dictionary's definition of a human being is 'A bi-pedal primate member of the family of Homo Sapiens'.

But do any of us really know what a bird or human being truly is?

This descriptive labelling does not begin to touch the core subtlety, emotional complexity and infinite potential of the human being's experience, any more than our language based labelling of 'a bird' 'tree' 'dolphin' 'mountain' touches the essence and resonance of that life form.

Looking out on the world and seeing a series of objects that are labelled and categorised does little to get to the heart of matter – to the pulse of life.

So how did we get to just label and constrict life into different categories? What perceptions and awareness are we losing with this mental filing system?

If we are to make a quantum shift whilst Pluto transits through Capricorn, we will need to peel back our current vision of 'seeing' life and look with fresh eyes at our true potential within it.

Chapter 4

The Underlying Blueprint

'Enclosed and safe within its central Heart nestles the seed perfection....the seed is waiting'

Walt Whitman *Writer and Poet*

All potential comes from a seed. The astrological natal chart is an x-ray of the seed waiting to fulfil its highest purpose – its fullest potential.

For each of us, whilst on Earth, our seed, the planetary blueprint that we embody at the time of our birth, is developed through beautifully orchestrated planetary cycles that infuse and enfold us.

At present, there are many belief systems as to why we embody a particular 'seed' or energetic patterning. Scientific knowledge speaks of genetic inheritance, mystical tradition says it is karmic, many say it is just chance.

No one would dispute, however, that we all have individual experiences and reactions during our formative years and, indeed, throughout our lives, which colour our perceptions.

For the first months, prior to speech, the underpinning astrological blueprint informing the seed can be seen primarily from the cycles of the Moon around the Earth, held within the light of the Sun feeding into our deepest unconsciousness. The astrological chart shows the likely underlying nurturing patterns that will be present for us in these early months, and which will unconsciously inform us of our 'safety' or otherwise within the environment.

As children we are forming neurological pathways from the moment that we are born and indeed during the period within the womb.

Our physical brain is basically composed of three parts, a triune system.

The seed of our human brain is the Brain Stem, or Reptilian Brain, which is the oldest part of the brain. This part of our brain is the brain found within reptiles and lizards. It has to do with maintaining body function and also with the basic drive of survival and territorial instinct.

The Limbic part, or Mammalian Brain, which is the second layer, or middle part of our brain, links to the autonomic nervous system and it too has to do with self-preservation, like the Reptilian system, but the Limbic Brain is also responsible for the development of emotions and memory, as well as for a sense of past present and future.

As the Mammalian brain links into the Neo Cortex, which is the third part of the brain, overlaying the other two, the range of emotions becomes ever more complex and subtle.

The Neo cortex, is divided into two hemispheres, the left, which is the most recently developed is for linear and rational thought, language and information and the right for spatial creative activity

The electrical current generated by the brain can be measured by means of an EEG (electro-encephalogram), which measures the frequency of the electrical current and these frequencies are grouped into four basic categories.

In our earliest months, touch, gentleness and loving security allows us to flow into a resonance that creates the foundation for building neurological pathways.

Looking at the table that follows you will see how the different 'brain' state rhythms operate and when they first start to appear.

Developmental Brain Patterns 0-12+

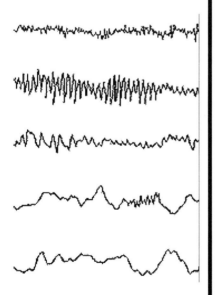

BETA 5+ years
Alert/Hardworking
Neo Cortex

ALPHA 1$^1/_2$ years
Relaxed/Reflecting
Neo Cortex/Limbic

THETA 3-6months
Drowsy/Ideating
Early Limbic

DELTA 0+
Sleeping/Dreaming
Brain Stem

DELTA 0+
Dreamless sleep
Brain Stem

During the first few weeks of our life as infants, each of us is perceiving life through a screen that is scientifically measured as Delta waves within the brain. These waves oscillate around 0.5 and 4.0 Hz.

As the weeks progress we begin to move into the Theta Range of brain 'activity', linking into the first cycle of Mercury, but this early period of life is still one in which the brain is in a calm vegetative state of rest and we are working from a sensory perspective of our surroundings. We have no factual data, or labels, to interfere with our perceptions, the neo cortex has yet to be developed and, like a sponge, we absorb all that is going on around us.

It is into this unconscious field that all that occurs is stored and held. Over the next months we begin to develop, sounds and speech, emotional interaction, and physical mobility. The cycles of Mercury, Venus and Mars begin to interact within us and our brain patterns become more active and take on an Alpha resonance.

In a relaxed state, as children, we fall into Theta Alpha states with ease – sensations, feelings, imagination, dreaming and creativity are all heightened.

It is often around the age of three to four that we may speak of imaginary friends, see things that our parents do not, or gaze up at a star and feel as if it is our home.

Without the boundaries of 'agreed' belief patterns many children do express these thoughts. It seems that the child may be able to see more fields than just our very defined visual spectrum.

Too often as children, we are just humoured with the thought that we will grow out of it and indeed we invariably do, for with education our neo cortex is stimulated and we enter into the Beta range of brain state awareness. With the advent of the first Saturn square around six and a half we learn take on a more conservative reality of 'agreed' consciousness, belief and consensus.

Our thoughts become more confined and the devic elemental kingdom of the 'little folk' and 'friends' begins to fade from view as we enter formal education.

You may think the young child's vision is just fanciful, but an experiment was done a few years ago which might raise some questions.

A group of people, at Harvard University, were asked to watch a video of a basket ball game. The group was asked to observe the team wearing white shirts and to count the number of passes made by them during the game.

At the end of the game they were asked to record their findings, which they did. They were then asked if they had seen a gorilla that had come into the hall during the game.

It turned out that around half had failed to spot a woman dressed in a gorilla suit who walked slowly across the scene for nine seconds, even though this extra player had passed between the other players and stopped to face the camera and beat her chest - it had just not been consciously registered by them.

Their 'Beta' induced brain states had been so focussed on the task in hand that they had screened out any extraneous information and yet on an unconscious level, at the level of Delta, Theta, Alpha, everything, including the Gorilla, will have been recorded within each of them.

This experiment would seem to clearly show, that the way we use our brain defines our field of vision and experience.

From the age of six through to twelve our brain patterns are focussed to moving between Beta and Alpha during waking hours and back to Theta Delta at night.

An immense amount of energy goes into the building of language and numeracy all reflected within the educational focus on the 3 R's at this time feeding into our surface mind. By the time we reach young adulthood we are primarily seeing the world through Beta perception.

Beta brain states, ranging from 14-30Hzs and upwards link to conscious alertness, active thinking and also, potentially, to stress, for if our focus remains too much within the Beta range stimulating, the left neo-cortex, without the ability to unwind, then it is at this point that we may be beginning to enter a gradual slide on the slippery slope towards disease. For it is in the higher Beta wavelengths that the fight or flight response is triggered and cortisol, known as the stress hormone, is produced.

What is interesting is that it is during early childhood that we have access to the healthiest levels of brainwaves.

When we enter Alpha, we are in a 'Super learning' state and when going deeper into Theta states of consciousness we access advanced states of creativity and healing.

For the first few weeks of our lives all of us are permanently flowing in a Delta consciousness (the slowest brain waves) and it has now been proved that this level of consciousness releases large quantities of healing growth hormone.

It is, of course, the time of major cellular growth, for a child, but it would also seem to indicate that when we access into these levels of brainwave we have the capacity to restore cellular damage. Just as lizards have the ability to re-grow their tails when they become damaged, so too, it would appear, we have the same potential for cellular regeneration stored within our own brain stems.

These unconscious, lower brains states are the seed bed from which we can develop the faculties of telepathy, clairvoyance and intuition – have the ability to think and see outside of the box – and also have the potential to access cellular regeneration and healing - natural gifts waiting to be developed and used.

The development of our neo-cortex is a vital component of our evolution as human beings, however, when it comes to dominate our focus and our thinking becomes too narrow, linear, or judgmental, then we may well be missing the picture.

It is Delta/Theta states of consciousness that are entered into by advanced meditators and which we, as children, have a natural access into. These are the states of consciousness that interlink and weave the mind and body deeply together.

Our bodies have an innate intelligence, for housed within each cell there is a storehouse of information and potential waiting to be accessed.

When we regain our natural ability to flow seamlessly and consciously between these brain states then we have the potential to enter into a unified field of 'Gamma' consciousness, which expands the third dimensional field, to create what might be called, spiritual enlightenment or supra consciousness. Our link to the Cosmos lies within our deepest unconsciousness.

In this field of consciousness we return to a state of innocence and purity. Young children have this innate sense of interconnection with all that they experience, for they interpret life, prior to speech, through their bodies' sensory capacity, uncluttered by mental chatter or judgment.

This clear field of perception may well give a whole new perspective to the words 'Unless you become like little children you cannot enter the Kingdom of Heaven'

Chapter 5

The Journey of Integration

"Enlightenment doesn't occur from sitting around visualizing images of light, but from integrating the darker aspects of the Self into the conscious personality."

Carl Jung *Psychoanalyst and Writer*

Rather like a computer chip, the astrological chart holds an infinite amount of knowledge within its circular seed, waiting to be revealed, experienced and understood as we journey through life on Planet Earth – our home.

It is such a gift to be on Planet Earth. The sights, sounds and sensations of being on Earth are wondrous. From the sound of bird song – light sparkling on the ocean - a crimson golden sky at sunset – holding a new born child – the fragrance of a rose - snowflakes falling silently to the ground - stars glistening in an indigo night sky - to the smell of freshly cut grass – all these are just but a tiny glimpse of the myriad of kaleidoscopic impressions that can speak to us all of a beauty that uplifts, surrounds and unites us on this Planet.

This beauty can touch our hearts in ways beyond words and has the potential to open us, to let go of resistances, to enter into mystical experience, leading us into other levels of awareness where all is interconnected and there is no sense of separation.

Whether we instinctively experience this harmony, or not, links intimately with our earliest childhood memories and our sense of openness and interconnection to the world around us.

From the following Table it is easy to see the profound effect the Moon cycle has upon each of us in our earliest months. It is during our deepest Delta unconscious phase that the cycles of the Moon around the Earth will have completed three Lunations, prior to Mercury completing its first return.

During these first three cycles, the Moon will have aspected each of the planets in the natal chart and will have activated the midpoints of all of the planets many times before any of the other planets have had any real imprint.

This is why the Moon's cycle is such an intrinsic element in our journey of integration.

Over the first two years of life the Moon will have orbited the Earth twenty-six times – overlaying the impressions, feelings, unconscious sensory and behavioral reactions which become the instinctive belief patterns of who we believe ourselves to be, based on our earliest family memories.

These impressions and beliefs are laid down and stored up within our subtle energetic system and endocrine system, reflecting and informing our underlying brain pattern activity, which in turn is informing our conscious, unconscious and cellular systems.

Throughout our lives, the cycles of the transiting planets, as they interact with the natal chart blueprint, continue to reaffirm the unconscious basic characteristics of these early months, unless consciously reviewed.

UNCONSCIOUS AND CONSCIOUS DEVELOPMENT
(Periods of Primary Focus)

DELTA /THETA linking into ALPHA
0-2 years   Absorbing information – R brain predominating
Moon   }   26 orbits of Earth/ link to Universal Field
Earth   }   2 orbits of Sun / Vitality/Pranic/etheric/field
Mercury }   8 orbits of Sun / CNS/movement/speech
Venus   }   3 orbits of Sun / Emotional/feeling response
Mars   }   1 orbit of Sun / Fight/flight reflex

THETA/ALPHA linking into BETA
2-6 years   Imagination – both R & L brain - R predominant
Moon   }   53 orbits of Earth/continuing imprint from 0-2 yrs
Earth   }   4 orbits of Sun/Pranic field feeding Light Body
Mercury }   16 orbits of Sun/CNS/speech development
Venus   }   6 orbits of Sun/Relationship skills developing
Mars   }   2 orbits of Sun/Ego/Will/Terrible 2's syndrome
Jupiter } $^1/_2$ orbit of Sun/Growth physical & consciousness

ALPHA/BETA WAVES
6-12 years   Reflective Consciousness - R & L brain operating
Saturn   } $^1/_4$> orbit of Sun around 6-7 yrs seals in the early
               imprints at first Saturn square. Clairvoyants say a
               fine mesh overlays the chakra points at this time
Moon   }   Moon cycle continues underlying blueprint,
Earth   }   but L brain becomes predominant. The cycles
Mercury }   of Earth/Mercury/Venus/Mars/Jupiter and Saturn
Venus   }   as they interconnect within a chart are the
Mars   }   basic building blocks of personality
Jupiter }   1 orbit of Sun / Growth/puberty/expansion

BETA/ALPHA (**GAMMA** potential)
12+   Alert focussed mind – L brain predominant

(After infancy we link into Delta/Theta waves primarily during
periods of sleep – Theta/Alpha during creativity or meditation)

It is not only our closest family environment that informs our unconsciousness for the Moon also links each of us into the universal field of the collective unconsciousness and, rather like a hard disk in the computer, over time this disk has become overloaded and corrupted.

Where once there would have been a clean and clear conduit between the harmonic resonances of the Sun, Moon and planetary orbits flowing down to Earth, now there is background static, for not a thought or feeling is ever lost and these subtle resonances have created another layer of information that separates us from the pure light and consciousness of Source.

All that has ever been felt, thought or experienced is stored and resonates within this layer of the quantum energetic field. These thought forms and feelings have become the human group unconsciousness and so each of us, as children, and indeed as adults, have the potential to link into the "Good the Bad and the Ugly" that is subtly resonating through the quantum field.

This resonance, over time becomes the automatic pilot, the 'radio station' we come to listen to and believe in. It is within this multi layered compost that each seed has to take root and grow. Our evolution individually and en masse, has to do fundamentally with the 'radio station' we choose to tune into.

Rather like the Large Hadron Collider in Geneva, we are all participating in particle acceleration as we spiral through time and space around the Solar System.

For as we each take on the task of clearing and transforming the negative or limited patterns of fear, guilt, shame and anger, held within each of us, as well as, within the group collective of humanity, we raise the resonance of the morphogenetic, holographic field that flows through us all.

As the background vibration/resonance rises, emotional and mental patterns such as fear and guilt etc. will eventually no longer manifest as their resonance will fall below the manifesting consciousness grid spectrum.

The energies which came from fear and ignorance will be utilized in other ways. We do not have to keep repeating the patterns of the past – we can consciously choose another path.

Our thoughts and feelings are highly creative and becoming more so with each passing year.

So rather than giving away our peace, power and trust to a fear about an upcoming Saturn transit, by labeling it difficult or malefic we need to clear the script that has produced such thought forms.

Saturn's resonance within our subtle system does indeed slow us down for a time, can put us under pressure, create a sense of isolation and the resonance may drop, but this is to put us in touch with areas of our life that we have chosen to overlook and disassociate from. During a Saturn transit we may have to face hidden fears and become more self-accountable,

These fears may be brought to the surface by some tangible, physical pain or event, in order that we may look again at what is still fueling our fears and lack of balance.

In working with Saturn and our bodies' wisdom, we have the opportunity to step beyond that limitation, ultimately finding harmony, understanding and peace.

From this perspective a Saturn transit is positive. The Saturn cycle is intimately connected to the development and harmonization of the physical, emotional and mental bodies, three levels of personal consciousness, that when integrated lead to soul consciousness.

All is working for our highest good. All is working to release us from low level resonance that has kept us tuned to a particular radio station which is past its sell by date.

Eckhart Tolle in his book 'The Power of Now' refers to this low level resonance as the 'emotional pain body' through which we react to the outside world.

Saturn's Developmental Cycle

Period	Development of Consciousness
0-7	Physical Body
7-14	Emotional Body
14-21	Mental Body
21-28	Soul Body
Cycle Repeat	28/29-56/58 and 56/58-84/86. Exact cycle period depends upon n.Saturn placement and retrograde movements
Sub Period	Each period is subdivided into five sections which repeat throughout the larger cycle
0 - 9 months	Water element kidney energy *integration*
9 ^{m} - 2 1/2 yrs	Wood element liver *movement*
2 1/2 - 4 yrs	Fire element heart *communication enthusiasm*
4 - 5 1/2 yrs	Earth element stomach spleen *creativity*
5$^{1/2}$ - 7 yrs	Metal element air lungs *to give wings to*

The pain body is the accumulation of past experiences and belief patterns stored in the unconscious of each of us and held by humanity as a whole, within the group unconscious.

It is the pain body that is creating the distortion not Saturn or any other orbiting planet.

The subtle resonances flowing down through the Cosmos are pure potential, and our role, whilst embodied is to clear our tape/pain body of negative imprints, in order to house clarity, so that we may become positively co-creative with the Cosmos.

For the Cosmos is for us – not against us.

Chapter 6

Reawakening

'It's exhilarating to be alive in a time of awakening consciousness; it can also be confusing, disorienting and painful'

Adrienne Riche *Poet*

Over the last three hundred years or so we have evolved and developed our level of consciousness, seemingly becoming more intelligent, more knowledgeable, more ingenious and yet paradoxically at the same time, it appears, emptier.

As we have focussed our attention on exploring physical reality and passing on the facts to generation after generation, our neo-cortex has become more and more stimulated and developed.

Having spent these last centuries, through our education, exploring material reality to the nth degree it is little wonder that we have become such a materialistic society.

Science, medicine and mathematics have all flourished during this period and have been a very valuable contribution to our lives.

However, sadly, they have flourished, at the expense of splintering away from the wisdom of past ages and this splintering and separation has created a deep inner rift and polarization within the psyche which is now manifesting through a society which appears, on many levels, to have lost its way.

There are many blessings to be received through the advancement of knowledge and the benefits of a more comfortable material existence, but if we forget our roots and these benefits come at the expense of 'amnesia' then they will be at a very high cost.

But, luckily, the Cosmos is here to wake us up.

For each time we 'discover' a new planetary body, our field of reference and belief patterns are interrupted, challenged, expanded and finally integrated.

The arrival of Uranus, the higher octave of Mercury, into our consciousness found the old order interrupted and challenged, reflected on a group level, by the Declaration of the American War of Independence and the French Revolution.

Freedom as an ideology became a prime focus.

When Neptune, the higher resonance of Venus appeared some one hundred years later, we had the potential to balance this rapid rate of mental stimulus, with a more humane emotional understanding of how we might create a freer society in a real sense. We are still working at it.

With each discovery we are given the opportunity to consciously work with the energy and to take self-responsibility for the choices that we make

To work constructively with the outer planetary energy of Uranus and Neptune, we have to have integrated the essence of Mercury and Venus, the lower octaves of Uranus and Neptune. This requires that we take personal responsibility for our thoughts and feelings, both on the conscious and unconscious levels – quite a task.

In just the same way, with the discovery of Pluto in 1930, we are being given the opportunity to work with the higher octave of Mars – to become empowered – and to take personal responsibility for our actions.

The greatest gift we can give to ourselves and to each other is to become consciously aware of what we are thinking and feeling. For our thoughts and feelings are the 'glue' that hold us in a particular state of resonance. Fear, shame, guilt, all have a vibrational rate - just as joy, peace, bliss equally resonate along the emotional spectrum.

The great gift that we have as astrologers, is that In a very practical way, we can observe what is going on in the subtle energetic light system of individuals, for we have a direct access and insight into this quantum field through the chart.

As such we can see when planetary aspects may be putting the energetic subtle system under stress, individually and en masse. When the resonance may drop, when the endocrine system is likely to be challenged and as a consequence the immune system can be depleted, creating emotional, mental difficulties and potential cellular disease.

In working with this knowledge we can assist others at times of stress and confusion.

The distorted information, fears, low resonance, energetic disturbance can be addressed and cleared, creating clarity and a purer, expanded connection with the Universal Energy Field.

Vibrational medicine, such as homeopathy, acupuncture, reflexology, kinesiology etc aid greatly, as does meditation, prayer, yoga, sound and colour therapies as each feed directly into the subtle energetic system, helping the body to come into balance during times of planetary realignments.

But the task of becoming self aware of how thoughts and feelings are affecting the vibrational state of our well being, and the environmental field that we all share, can only come through personal growth and focus.

It seems we have the potential to Become of Age.

To do this we need to have integrated our basic personality, and then have developed and matured through the cycles of Jupiter and Saturn.

With this 'anchoring' we can then step into the field of higher resonance, consciously, and start to activate the positive qualities of the transpersonal planets that we have come to experience and to express in this lifetime.

Over vast periods of time we have been evolving to express this enlightened frequency.

The wake up call to step into this field was sounded by Pluto just over 70 years ago, for we are being asked to handle power – power that is imbued with loving kindness and wisdom.

Pluto's resonance is of such a depth and intensity that it brings to the surface emotional and mental imprints that have remained beneath our conscious radar. It seems to resonate to the earliest unconscious memories contained within the brain stem and our cellular form – linking us back into aeons of time.

Pluto has been bringing us face to face with our individual and group unconscious power choices as they manifest in our world.

In the first two decades after Pluto's arrival we witnessed in our global mirror the Second World War, the dropping of the Atomic Bomb on Hiroshima, the creation of Israel and Palestine, the standoff over the Suez Canal, the start of the Cold War with Russia, the power of oil, along with Mahatma Gandhi's vision for a peaceful transition of power and the creation of a new country, Pakistan.

Then as we moved into the 1960's we began to witness a flowering of a different consciousness. As Uranus moved ever closer to Pluto through the early part of the 1960's, Earth witnessed the beginning of a shift in the group conscious.

There was a group, root desire to see change and peace on this planet. Like a warm soft breeze this desire for change was tangible, it was as if we had stepped into another world and the fashion and music of that time reflected this upsurge of life and colour.

In a more profound sense, the mass demonstrations, by the CND, that took place in 1960 in England at Aldermaston, to 'Ban the Bomb'; in America, in 1967, to stop the War in Vietnam and the rally by Martin Luther King in 1968 to end Racial discrimination, all highlighted this regeneration of spirit.

Within a decade Chiron was to come and join the awakening. Since 1977 Chiron's arrival on the scene, has assisted in this accelerated shift of consciousness, for Chiron embraces both the material, physical boundary of Saturn's orbit and the outer planetary orbital space which Uranus inhabits.

Chiron's resonance bridges the physical and metaphysical realms, healing, synthesising and fusing particles of both matter and light within the physical body.

Since Chiron's arrival in the 70's there has been an immense increase in our understanding and interest in all things to do with vibrational sub atomic energy.

The morphogenetic or holographic field, auras, the chakra system, vibrational medicine, energetic healing, inter-dimensional fields and wormholes – all have come into mainstream awareness.

Both Pluto and Chiron enfold and cocoon the orbital paths of the planets. They bring a synthesis and integration to the individual resonances, bringing a fusion that takes us into another level of understanding that has the potential to turn a cog on the cosmic spiral.

On 30th December 1999 Chiron and Pluto came together in the sky at 11 degrees 22 of Sagittarius to commence a new cycle – the first cycle that we have had the opportunity to be consciously aware of.

In Dane Rudhyar's book 'An Astrological Mandala' which gives a channelled image of each of the degrees of the zodiac, he describes this degree of the zodiac as: 'A flag turns into an eagle; the eagle into a chanticleer saluting the Dawn.'

The keynote of which is 'The spiritualization and promotion of a New Age by minds sensitive to its *precursory* manifestation' He goes on to say 'It urges us to bring our noblest ideals to actual life through the power of the spiritual will'

This particular cycle will end on 13th April 2068 when both Pluto and Chiron come together again at 2 Aries 18. Here Dane Rudhyar says of this degree 'The cameo profile of a man suggesting the shape of his country'.

He goes on to say '...the individualizing person finds power and inner security in realizing his essential identity with the section of the Universe in which he operates. He, and it seems to his consciousness, is united in a cosmic-planetary process......the individual person can become truly, not only an image and representation of the Whole of his natal environment (Local, Planetary and eventually Cosmic) but an agent through whom the Whole may express itself in an act of creative resonance and outpouring. This is the avatar ideal.'

So what is only a knowing and awareness for a relative few at the start of this Pluto Chiron cycle of 1999, becomes, over the 70 year orbital period a possibility for many.

And what is the avatar's ideal? It is to live an empowered life, in peace and harmony with all beings. It is to have Spirit and Soul fully embodied, Light in Matter, and to be co-creative with the Universe giving the potential to manifest, what we have previously called miracles.

Pluto and Chiron over shadow and over light the cosmic field of our Solar System. Consciously passing through these cycles marks a profound time of regrouping and realigning, for they oversee and underwrite the cleansing of the consciousness.

They take us into an awareness way beyond a personality, into the core of our essence, into all that is held within our unconscious field where countless gifts await us.

It is our unconscious imprinting that holds the key to our state of being and it is through the integration of Chiron's and Pluto's resonance that we may heal personal and ancestral wounds and restructure our energetic system, giving us new pathways to explore, and bringing us into closer alignment to our true purpose.

Chiron's gift, even though initially it may create much disturbance and pain, is to bring to light that which we have chosen to disassociate from and which is creating such underlying distress and fear.

And what is it that we have disassociated from – it would appear - we have forgotten who we are.

Chapter 7

To the Heart of the Matter

'There is a Light that shines beyond all things on Earth, beyond us all; beyond the Heavens, beyond the highest the very biggest Heaven – this is the Light that shines in our Heart'

Chandogya Unpanishad

We are miraculous.

As human beings we are an exceptionally sensitive Life Form. Receiving, transmitting and recording the experiences of our lives through a multitude of levels, sensations and nuances. We are bombarded with visual data that would take thousands of computer processors to handle the same work load that is done by one human brain.

Scientists tell us that our retina, which is about one centimetre in diameter and has some hundred million neurons making up its nerve tissue, sends light images to the brain, via the optic nerve which is a million stranded fibre cable.

The power of a single human brain in terms of memory capacity is phenomenal.

As a living, breathing, feeling, human being, we assimilate and translate the energetic patterns, flowing through the Cosmos, nanosecond by nanosecond through our subtle energetic bodies.

For held within our physical form, our energetic subtle light body, or chakra system, as described by mystics and clairvoyants, encodes our everyday impressions, reactions, feelings, thoughts and actions as they are played out moment by moment. But over and above all of this amazing infrastructure and neurological wiring we each have a hidden gift that is beyond price.

This gift which is enfolded deep within each cell's consciousness is the resonance of pure light that is contained within matter.

It is through the evolution of planetary cycles that this hidden gift can come 'to light'. Think of each planet like a tuning fork, as creating a particular resonance, note or colour, through its unique vibrational field within our subtle energetic system.

Each planet's underlying resonance subtly connecting through the morphogenetic field into our auras through the etheric field, feeding into the physical, and stimulating the emotional, mental and spiritual faculties that we each possess – to bring us into a greater potential, synthesis and balance. This resonance is then reflected in our auric field, our brain patterning and our cellular system and becomes the screen through which we interpret life.

Put very simplistically, at present, our energetic system which underpins our atomic structure is basically composed of seven primary states of awareness, each is interconnected to the other and each has a particular spectrum of resonance and consciousness.

Just like the twelve houses in a chart or our different brain states, each of the chakras has a specific resonance spectrum and function, but each is intimately interconnected, and interdependent with each other.

The chakras store and expel energy – permanently fluctuating and resonating with each thought, feeling and sensation. Heat sound and light, as well as the general health of the body will create fluctuations within this energetic field.

There are many books written on this subject, so this is just a brief overview of the subtle system. The following diagram describes the basic outline of our energetic system illustrating seven major chakras that interlink the subtle energetic system with the physical body and the environmental field of our Solar System.

The Seven Primary Chakras Overlaying the Endocrine Glands

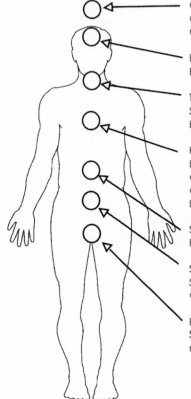

Crown Chakra/Pineal/Sahasrara Connection to Universal Consciousness

Brow Chakra/Pituitary/Ajna Third Eye/clairvoyance/intuition

Throat Chakra/Thyroid/Vishuddi Seat of communication/link between Heart and mind

Heart Chakra/Thymus/Anahatta Balancing point for the three lower chakras and three upper chakras/Unconditional Love/Universal Heart

Solar Plexus/Pancreas/Manipura Personal power centre/personality

Sacral Chakra/Ovary Gonad/ Swadhistana/ Personal likes and dislikes/sense of belonging

Root Chakra/Adrenals/Muladhara Sense of survival/fright/flight/fight/ reflex

The first three chakras relate to the material world, the physical body, to subjective thoughts/feeling and beliefs, to likes and dislikes - whilst the upper three chakra functions have to do with subtler objective/higher mental/spiritual integration. The numbering system is not hierarchical as each chakra is part of an integral whole.

For men, the 1st 3rd and 5th chakras predominate, as males are energetically linked positively to these three. The 2nd, 4th and 6th chakras of the feeling emotional function are more internalised as these have a negative charge within their auric field.

For women, it would appear, the polarity is reversed – the 1st 3rd and 5th chakras are negatively charged – and the 2nd 4th and 6th chakras are positively charged.

The Heart Chakra or, Anahatta, balances and integrates the lower three chakras with the upper three chakras for both male and female. When energetically focussed within the Anahatta centre, the positive and negative polarity of the chakra system for males and females becomes less polarised.

The male is able to take on his nurturing, feeling, intuitive capacity and the female is able to embrace her independence and power. When we are looking for 'our missing other' we are experiencing life through a subjective viewpoint and we are linking into a particular vibrational spectrum.

The four major asteroids of Juno, Ceres, Pallas Athena and Vesta play a fundamental role in assisting in the integration of the male/female balance – in particular

Juno links to the Sacred Marriage to the union of male and female within for both men and women.

When fused through the heart, we are able to integrate both the positive and negative charged polarity of our own chakra system – no longer projecting our 'missing' part out on to others,

Just like the colour spectrum in which we can only access certain colours because of our eyes' physical ability to only perceive within a range of frequency – so too are our physical emotional and mental experiences equally limited to the particular range of vibrational frequency operating through our chakra system.

Mankind has, for generations, lived and died from a 'reality awareness' coming fundamentally from the three lower chakras and this has created many limiting thought forms.

When we are born, we inherit the field of thoughts that surround us and also those that we bring through past lives/ancestral lineage.

Spiritual wisdom says, however, that through each lifetime and, indeed, through each experience in life, we have the potential to evolve through this cosmic field of consciousness, from a personal agenda towards a Universal Consciousness, leaving behind fear and ignorance, raising our vibrational resonance and in so doing increasing the light quotient within our cellular structure.

As we learn to evolve and mature as individuals and as a species, we eventually move into the Anahatta, or Heart Chakra, as our primary focus and in this state of resonance we create a field that assists our higher consciousness or Soul to be embodied. This is the pathway of all traditional spiritual wisdom.

It is whilst we are experiencing life through the focus and resonance of the subjective lower centres that we find the outer planetary energies disruptive and traumatic. Unexpected events, challenges and stresses occur, creating tension and pain.

However, when we are centred and balanced within the heart chakra then our experiences of these outer planetary energies are expressed more co-creatively and constructively

With the latest cycle of Uranus and Neptune, which began in February 1993, our subtle energetic systems, via the pituitary and pineal glands, are being fine tuned to bring us into connection with a higher resonances of thought and feeling.

As the crown chakra is stimulated, this is reflected through the brow, throat and heart chakras creating a mind/heart connection, a clearer resonating and unified field that will enable more enlightened states of consciousness to be embodied.

When thoughts and feelings are linked into Universal Consciousness our auric field resonates at a far lighter and higher frequency, our brain waves, via the triune system, come into higher states of awareness and harmony and we, in turn, feed this resonance back into the morphogenetic field for all.

Each of us is an integral part of this Field of Light, and through this Field, there is a symbiotic evolutionary exchange that has been occurring since time began.

Chapter 8

Remembering

'Come with me now, Pilgrim of the stars, for our time is upon us and our eyes shall see the far country and the shining cities of infinity which the wise men knew in ages past, and shall know again in the ages yet to be.'

Robert Burnham *Poet*

Much is forgotten through the passage of time.

It is within ancient traditions, however, that we can trace our ancestral, astronomical and astrological roots for the civilizations of Babylonia, Persia, Egypt, China, India, Greece and Rome have all been central to the accumulation of knowledge that has been passed down to us.

These civilizations were far more interested in the stellar landscape and the passage of time, than our present day focus on individual horoscopes. They had abilities and talents that we seem to have forgotten.

From the Egyptian pyramids, to the wonders of Machu Picchu in Peru the civilizations had an understanding of building way beyond our capabilities today.

There is much mystery surrounding these monumental structures. Both societies had a strong astronomical background – Egypt's linking closely to Orion and Sirius and the Inca's of Peru to the Pleiades.

It has often been suggested that there was an astro-physically advanced ancient culture which built these amazing structures and then disappeared, along with their advanced ideas.

The Egyptian and Inca civilizations were not the only astro-physically gifted culture.

The Mayan culture, from Mesoamerica, (Mexico, Guatemala and Honduras) is also known for its monumental architecture and also for their mastery in astronomy and mathematics.

They have acted as Time Keepers for us all as we travel around our Galaxy.

As the keepers of the Cosmic abacus, the Mayas had a complicated method of keeping track of time, based on many separate astrological calendars.

The Mayan calendars were derived from those of their predecessors, the Olmec whose culture dates back over 3,000 years.

Long before the invention of the instruments of 16th century Europe, this Central American civilization managed to calculate a solar year of 365.2420 days - just out by 0.0002 on our present day calculations.

This calculation of 365 days, known as the 'Vague Year' along with a cycle of 260 days known as the 'Sacred Year' are the two main calendars used by the Maya.

The Sacred Calendar or Tzolk'in – links to the cycle of the Pleiades and is referred to as the 'Long Count'

In the sacred books of the Maya it is written that they came from the Pleiades – this belief has been passed on down through the ages to this day.

The Maya had a personal understanding and vision of the Cosmos that is breathtaking in its scope and certainly one that is astro-physically gifted.

They knew the location of the centre of the Milky Way long before the advent of any telescope.

They called this point in space 'The Galactic Butterfly' or Hunab Ku. According to Maya tradition, this point in space is the gateway or portal to other Galaxies. Hunab Ku is the Creator, the consciousness which organized all the ephemeral dust into stars, planets and solar systems. For the Mayas, Hunab Ku is constantly giving birth to new stars and it gave birth to our own Sun and to planet Earth.

They also believe, that it is from this centre that all was directed through periodic bursts of energy that consciously create and organise all that occurs within our Galaxy.

Many thousands of years later, our present day astronomers have now found evidence that there is a whirling disc complete with a Black Hole at the centre of our Galaxy which is both swallowing and giving birth to stars.

So these star gazers of long ago held knowledge that is mystifying in its complexity of understanding.

In Maya tradition, there is a fundamental difference between the way that they perceived time, and how we understand time now, in that they did not see it as linear.

The Mayas believed essentially that time flows in a circle. There is a beginning and an end to things but there is a renewal at the end of the time cycle.

Mayan Cycles

1: Cellular Cycle	16.4 billion years
2: Mammalian Cycle	820 million years
3: Familial Cycle	41 million years
4: Tribal Cycle	2 million years
5: Regional Cycle	102,000 years
6: National Cycle	5125 years
7: Planetary Cycle	256 years
8: Galactic Cycle	12.8 years
9: Universal Cycle	0.72 years

The Mayan Cycle Table shows cycles within cycles, starting with the Cellular cycle which spans some 16.4 billion years down to the Galactic Cycle that encompasses 12.8 years then moving through to the Universal Cycle that covers just nine months or so.

According to their calculations, we are now passing through a 12.8 year Galactic Cycle which commenced on the 5th of January 1999 and which, according to their calculations, will end on the 21st of December 2012.

This 12.8 year cycle links to the time period when the Sun at the time of the Winter Solstice is steadily, year by year, transiting across the Galactic Equator close to the heart of the Galaxy – a location known as the 'Dark Rift in the Milky Way'.

This alignment occurs due to the Precession of the Equinoxes, which appears to move the Sun around the ecliptic against the fixed stars.

On December 21st 2012 at 11:11 GMT precisely, the Sun will hold still for a time, as it does on each Solstice and it will mark the closing phase of this transition across the Galactic Equator

What is fascinating is that many thousands of individuals, during the 1990's, to the present day, from around the world, have been prompted to 'pay attention' by seeing this 11:11 wake up call on their digital clocks, computers, radios etc.

Some may say that this is just chance, but others would say that it is a vital Galactic nudge - come what may the times we are traveling through ask that we all become far more conscious.

Having looked back at the cosmic clock – where does that leave us now as we pass through the Mayan Galactic Cycle leading up to the Solstice of 2012? One thing is for sure, the Maya astrologers have left us a large memo to remember the time that we are in.

It is a time of reconnection – a time when the Solar System and Planet Earth in particular connects deeply into the heart of the Milky Way Galaxy and just like a Cosmic combination lock as it clicks into place, we are about to start a new cycle, one that can bring us into Galactic consciousness and a profound evolutionary shift.

Chapter 9

Moving into the Soular System

"The day breaks through me. I am a window in the Universe for the nameless reality."

A.H. Almaas *Writer and Teacher*

So here we are on Planet Earth, our home, travelling through the Solar system and about to go through the cosmic checkout, a point in time and space that was recorded long, long ago. All of us embodied at this time on planet Earth volunteered to be here at this point in time and space.

Our space ship is perfectly on time, but are we?

The Mayas, the Incas and other indigenous and ancient civilizations on this planet had a deep sense of connection to not only the stars, but also to Mother Earth.

They saw themselves as intrinsically part and parcel of the world that surrounded them having a deep interconnection with spirit and nature.

Over the last centuries, many people, particularly, in the more prosperous regions of the world, have disconnected from the rhythms of the Earth and the Sky, becoming more and more, isolated and insulated from their ancestral spiritual roots and nature's gifts.

This isolation has grown progressively over the last decades for now we are surrounded by so many diversions. We can switch on a TV, or a computer, pick up a magazine or newspaper and be taken into a world that describes and circumscribes who we are at this point in time and space.

Like wall to wall carpeting there is little room for individual bare boards and clean space in which to discover who we might be without this pre-packaging - to rediscover the essence of who we really are without the script and outer veneer that we have created for ourselves.

It is time to reclaim our true potential – our ancestral inheritance. For right now we are being taken back to our ancestral roots and we are being given every help and assistance from the Cosmos to become more emotionally mature, more aware and to fast track into an awakening of consciousness that has been spoken of for thousands of years.

Since the 1970's we have had the opportunity to work with Pluto, the gatekeeper to Galactic Consciousness and Chiron, the first of the Centaurs to materialise, clearing and cleansing old patterns from within our cellular structure that would keep us held in low resonance and limited awareness.

Passing through the gateway and rings of Saturn, working with Uranus and Neptune, we embark upon another stage of our Galactic journey, as we enter into the landscape of the Centaurs.

The Centaurs carry a particular energetic. Chiron's initiatory pathway is acutely intense, it can feel as if our very spines are being turned to platinum to be strengthened and honed to carry this heightened vibratory essence.

Pholus and Nessus are such recent additions to our field of awareness and yet they appear at such a perfect time to maximise their potent message for radical change. Their energies take us into what appears as untamed consciousness – a force field which requires great internal balance – rather like a surfer on a Pacific wave we learn how to move and flow with this unknown experience.

The Centaurs mirror and reflect an evolutionary pathway that brings us into contact with instinctual behavioural patterns that resonate deep within our brain stems and cellular memory coming from our ancient ancestral past.

The Centaurs resonance has the potential to put us in touch with a level of instinctive consciousness that has been buried, controlled and or abandoned – pushed into the Shadow. We are given the opportunity to consciously balance and integrate this raw force field of light into our bodies and in so doing we link into unrefined primal energy that seems to activate and link us into our cerebellum and brain stems.

Passing through a transit of any of these Centaurs when they connect deeply into your chart, can create a sense that you and or the world have gone crazy. No amount of rational thought is going to sort out what is going on within and around you.

As your logical mind finally gives up the struggle you may find yourself being taken to another shore – a new horizon - which asks you to rest easy, to still the mind, and come into an alignment and embodiment with your Soul.

To handle this energy our focus needs to be centred within the Anahatta Heart Chakra and personal integrity and strength need to meld the raw force of the Centaurs with temperance, self responsibility and emotional maturity, for an alchemical process is occurring.

Saturn is the loadstone that allows for the alchemy of this pure raw energy to be forged and fused into higher consciousness. Lead turning to Gold. For although, at first, Saturn appears to block and hinder our personal drive, in effect our resonance is being taken into the Telluric realm, linking us deeply into the elemental Earth plane.

Chiron enfolds and fuses Saturn and Uranus into freeing and healing the mind. Pholus enfolds and fuses Saturn and Neptune into aligning the heart into another level of awareness and Nessus enfolds and fuses Saturn and Pluto into deepening and aligning with our will and purpose in life.

As the Centaurs weave their paths of light around Saturn and the outer planets we are spun into an awakening in which the Reptilian, Mammalian and Neo Cortex areas of our brain are all triggered - a switch has been thrown and we are awakening and lighting up dark recesses of the brain.

We may find ourselves pulled in all directions with an intensity that can strip us of our outer civilised veneer and penetrate and shock the central nervous system. Without a deep sense of self responsibility, held within the Saturnian archetype, and balanced within the heart, the resonance of the Centaurs can still create havoc, but they also open us up to a far vaster vision of our potential as human beings.

During a Centaur transit, our energetic body is being tweaked another degree - it is releasing the oldest ancestral memory patterns, from within the group consciousness.

Our energetic body is being refined and restructured, so that sensory, emotional and mental experiences can all be heightened and, those parts of our psyche that are trapped in a learnt pattern of behaviour, which is both stultifying and ultimately crucifying, will no longer be part of our energetic field.

Chiron is the key to the doorway of the Anahatta chakra. Within this heart focus, we, as human beings, are embodying the pivotal point – we become the balancing fulcrum of the Earth's elemental energies, uniting and interpenetrating with outer planetary cycles.

We are the conduits and bridge that link and fuse past and future, the deepest Earth plane with the purest Light.

Spiralling and stripping us of any false masks and inflated egos, or indeed deflated sense of self, the Centaurs encourage us to grow beyond a mentally based, dualistic consciousness formed from limited perspectives.

As we become aware of a much larger theatre that is being played out on planet Earth our energetic body shape shifts to hold this greater resonance within physical form and we enter into another level of consciousness, a consciousness that flows through the eighth chakra – the seat of our Soul.

This Eighth chakra is not a New Age concept, for in Mithraic teaching from around 1200 BC the Indo-Persian teachers spoke of seven gates leading to the eighth – the Bridal Chamber, the seat of the Soul, where Spirit and Soul align.

Today, clairvoyants and sensitives have described changes within the auric field, noticing a further chakra vortex, some 12 inches above the crown chakra, called the Soul Star, balancing out with another chakra, around one foot below the feet, called the Earth Star, which has become consciously operational in some individuals

As we open to greater and greater light input from the cosmos, flowing within our being, we require this extra anchoring and openness in order to integrate and balance these outer energies and it would appear to

The Soul and Earth Star Chakras

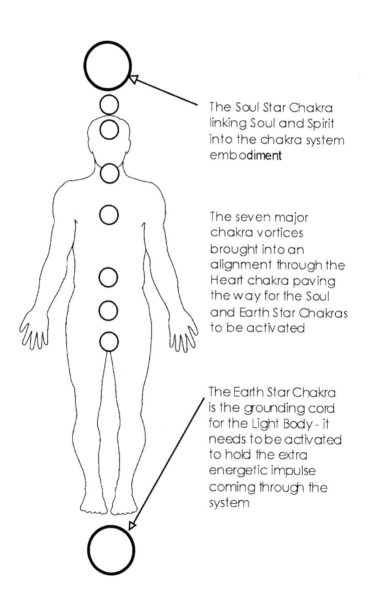

The Soul Star Chakra linking Soul and Spirit into the chakra system embodiment

The seven major chakra vortices brought into an alignment through the Heart chakra paving the way for the Soul and Earth Star Chakras to be activated

The Earth Star Chakra is the grounding cord for the Light Body - it needs to be activated to hold the extra energetic impulse coming through the system be the Centaurs resonance, uniting Saturn with Uranus Neptune and Pluto, that is allowing our energetic system to realign with Soular Consciousness.

And so it is that we find ourselves being ushered to the threshold of the Kuiper Belt where Pluto resides, the first of the 'planetary' bodies to bid us enter this unknown, expansive field which holds our initial stellar blueprint,

Chapter 10

Back to the Future

*'You didn't come into this world, you came out of it.
Like a wave in an ocean you are not a stranger here'*

A Watts *Professor of Biochemistry*

The Kuiper Belt is a vast disc of stellar dust extending some seven billion miles out beyond the orbit of Neptune. Scientists say that it is composed of the particles that were left over from forming our Solar System.

Pluto and all the other planetary bodies within the Kuiper field that orbit through this stellar cloud, link us back to the very beginning of time.

Little wonder then that Pluto's resonance initially shakes us up. For how else are we to break free from our self contained image and cocoon of who we think we are, as opposed to who we truly are, without a fundamental restructuring to the system to become more whole, true and alive.

Mystical traditions teach that we have gradually coalesced from light into matter - that we are spiritual beings, crystallised light in physical form and that we are connected through time and space with the elemental energies of the mineral, plant and animal kingdoms - all of which vastly pre-date the development of the human mental faculty.

The energetic of the Kuiper Belt has the capacity to link us into our deepest unconscious - into the Deep Feminine. Over many hundreds of years, this all encompassing creative, intuitive, unconscious Feminine power has been viewed with a mixture of fear, suspicion and cynicism, cast out as unreliable, or even evil, for unless everything could be proved, measured and quantified according to a 3rd dimensional mantra, then it has been disregarded.

This rapid and unprecedented focus on our neo-cortex over the last couple of centuries has been a vital part of our mental development as a species – what is crucial now, however, is whether we can bring a balance to this advanced mental state, with high level heart centred feeling, intuition and creativity - for without this realignment we become a lost, unbalanced and dangerous species.

The deep subconscious holds immense gifts for us all – it is the driving focus behind all of our experiences in life – it is the silent monitor that is expressing itself in all that we encounter whilst awake and asleep. So we need to link far more deeply into this power house that we all unconsciously breathe and live through.

Conscious Mind	Subconscious Mind
Volitional Sets goals, judges. Thinks abstractly.	**Habitual::** Monitors operation of the body. Thinks laterally
Time Bound Past and future	**Timeless:** Present time only
Limited Process Capacity: Short term memory– (approx 20 seconds) 1-3 events at a time Average 2,000 bits of information per second	**Expanded Processing Capacity** Long term memory, past experiences, attitudes, values and beliefs. 1000's of events at a time. An average of 4 billion bits of information per second

Two recent discoveries within this field of the Kuiper Belt have been Quaoar and Sedna, brought to light in October 2002 and November 2003. These Kuiper Belt messengers link us back to the creation myths, to the dawning of life.

Quaoar has been named after the creative force of the Tongva indigenous Indian tribe of South California. The Tongva people lived simplistically in an area that is now known as Los Angeles.

They believed that the Creator, Quaoar, sang and danced everything into being. The Sky, the Sun, the Earth and Moon, followed by the oceans, all came from this symphony and harmony.

According to their creation myth, at first there was Chaos and then when Quaoar, the creative spirit, saw the emptiness of this chaos he/she created Weiwot, the Sky God – then Chehoot – the Goddess of Earth and they between them created the Sun, Tamit, and the Moon, Moar. The Tongva saw everything as interconnected - a spirit flowing through all of creation.

The Shamanic tradition held by certain members within the tribes, was an integral part of their society. The indigenous tribes believed and, indeed, no doubt saw spirit/energy flowing through all of creation, for they spoke of a Great White Spirit, or Holy Ghost, that interpenetrates all of life.

Today, in the language of quantum physics, physicists would describe this Great White Spirit, as the interconnecting morphogenetic or holographic field underpinning all physical creation.

In just the same way, the concept of sound, as the basis for creation, held within the Tongva tribe is given credence today by modern day physicists. Professor Paolo de Bernadis, Physics Professor at the University of Rome, specialising in experimental astrophysics and cosmology, states 'The early Universe is full of sound waves compressing and rarefying matter and light, much like sound waves compress and rarefy air inside a flute or trumpet'

This sense of sound underpinning creative movement is also central to our astrological understanding, reflected in the thoughts of Pythagoras that 'There is geometry in the humming of the strings and there is music in the spacings of the spheres'

And so it is with the myth of Sedna too, that creation is seen as a multi layered living consciousness, for it speaks of inner layers within physical form. Sedna's story comes from the Inuit tribe – it embodies the theme of how the Feminine is sacrificed and forced underground into the deepest part of the ocean. The myth speaks of Sedna's pride and vanity that is transmuted and refined through this sacrifice.

In the giving of her life, Sedna gives birth to the earliest creatures of the ocean.

The Sedna myth closely follows the mystical tradition, that the Divine Feminine is to be found in all matter - the Divine Feminine that went into the deepest and darkest areas to hold and form life.

The Divine Feminine or 'Shekinah' meaning the 'Dwelling or settling place of God' refers to the perfect balance of Divine principle – the yin/yang, Ida/Pingali of mystical tradition which recognises this eternal balance of the polarities of masculine and feminine, light and dark, inner and outer, visible and invisible that flows through all of life. From the beginning of time, the Feminine principle, Matter/Love has held the Masculine principle of Consciousness/Light so that it might become embodied in physical form.

Quantum physicists understand that at the subtle sub- atomic level, matter and light are permanently interchanging, one into the other - the magnetic field holding the electrical impulse that fuses into matter and that they are one source, interdependent upon each other.

As humans, we seem to have forgotten this Natural Law of the balance of polarity that flows throughout life, but the primordial field that enfolds Quaoar and Sedna may well help us to remember, this cosmic harmony, of shamanic tradition as we consciously begin to integrate their resonance.

These resonances are the ancestral imprints upon our brain stem, they link us into the deepest unconsciousness – pre-mind – pre-thought, but they also offer the greatest precognition, for they link us into an instinctive, intuitive understanding of life beyond the purely linear, mental and rational.

The Shamanic pathways have never left the Earth, but now one shamanic pathway is reappearing on the planet with a 21st century scientific twist, in the shape of the work that is being carried out by Masaru Emoto, who has been demonstrating so clearly, through his beautiful crystal photographs, how the power of human thought combined with loving intention can work directly with elemental energy, clarifying, restructuring and restoring the purity of water within rivers and lakes.

Looking at these intricate, timeless photographs we are taken into a miniature world of exquisite geometry which radiates out a subtle message that speaks to our innermost soul.

We are asked to remember that we too are formed of water and we too can create, beautiful, intricate, crystal light geometry within our very being - healing, through loving intent - becoming the embodiment of liquid light.

On the soul's evolutionary journey, to become this 'Liquid Light,' Chiron and the Centaur Field take us through the 'local' shadow of our personal and joint misperceptions contained within Saturn's rings, to embody Uranian and Neptunian resonance, so that we may pass through the gateway of Pluto to obtain the gifts that await us as we access into Galactic consciousness.

To facilitate and to embody Galactic, Universal, Christos consciousness we need a profound shift of awareness.

Back in 1954 Albert Einstein said "A human being is part of the whole called by us, the Universe, a part limited in time and space. We experience ourselves, our thoughts and feelings as something separate from the rest - a kind of optical delusion of consciousness. This delusion is a kind of prison for us, restricting us to our personal desires and to affection for a few persons nearest to us.

Our task must be to free ourselves from the prison by widening our circle of compassion to embrace all living creatures and the whole of nature in its beauty. The true value of a human being is determined by the measure and the sense in which they have obtained liberation from the self. We shall require a substantially new manner of thinking if humanity is to survive."

From Ego to Soular Consciousness

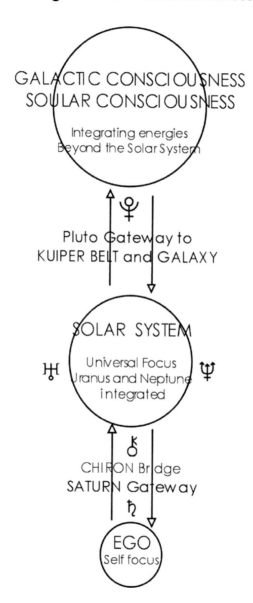

GALACTIC CONSCIOUSNESS
SOULAR CONSCIOUSNESS

Integrating energies
Beyond the Solar System

♇

Pluto Gateway to
KUIPER BELT and GALAXY

SOLAR SYSTEM

Universal Focus
Uranus and Neptune
integrated

♅   ♆

⚷

CHIRON Bridge
SATURN Gateway

♄

EGO
Self focus

Einstein echoes our astrological journey as we evolve through the boundary of Saturn, to integrate and embody Uranian, Neptunian and Plutonic resonance and onwards to the journey that we will all eventually embark upon – the journey of liberating ourselves from the confines of our own Solar limitation, recognising that we have the potential to be a part of a vast Galaxy, where our star, the Sun is just one of billions.

In a state of grace we embody this potential. When the mind and the heart are as one and stilled from judgment and comparison, when we embody an inclusive love for all Life and when we have the humility to recognise that Life is far more wondrous than we have conceived, then we may open the door to our next evolutionary spiral.

This is the journey of the Soul, as opposed to the personality, for it is the pure essence of the Soul which links us into Galactic consciousness.

This new evolutionary spiral, quantum leap, and reconfiguration, according to the Maya, clicks into place on 21st December 2012 and will continue to blossom and flower over the next centuries.

Right now and over these next few years, as we find ourselves once again, coming into an alignment with the Galactic Equator at the Winter Solstice, we need to let go of and, indeed, go beyond our individual mental egos, open our hearts to our incredible lineage as

From the Microcosm to the Macrocosm

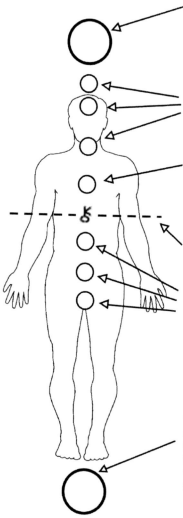

The Soul Star Chakra via Pluto's gateway connects us into the Kuiper Belt and on and out into Galactic Consciousness and Soul resonance with the Earth Star

The Crown Brow and Throat are balanced with the three lower chakras to reflect the Soul Star

The Heart centre takes on a higher resonance and is the focal point for this expanded energetic field

Chiron bridges the resonance of outer planetary energy with the Saturn boundary linking us into the Heart Chakra

The Root, Sacral and Solar Plexus Chakras aligned and balanced assisting the Brow and the Heart to unite so that the Throat Chakra can express the Unity of the Soul and Galactic Consciousness rather than a limited subjective and duality based consciousness

The Earth Star connects the energy of the 8th Chakra the Soul Star into the physical and links us into the brain stem and cerebellum - to our ancestral roots as Beings of Light.

human beings, through time and space and reunite with this cosmic connection, if we are to take our first footsteps into this virgin ground.

This is the potential shift of consciousness that the Mayas foresaw so many years ago and we here on Earth right now are the potential seeds of this future flowering.

Chapter 11

Completing the Circle

"Imagine what it would be like if you were able to come to the end of division within yourself and then come together with another, or many others, who had also done the same....that's miraculous because, in that, the inner spiritual revelation of oneness enters this world in the form of relationship. Only when you bring it into this world does the circle become complete. Heaven has come to Earth".

Andrew Cohen *Spiritual Teacher*

As human beings our greatest gift and equally, our Achilles heel, is our mental capacity. We have the power of thought, reason, assessment, analysis and judgment – only problem is, what are we basing our judgment upon?

Nine times out of ten, it will be from a Saturn boundary perspective. A subjective personal assessment of how things should be, could be, ought to be.

Mystical wisdom, however, teaches that everything is, in effect a reflection, a mirror to our own inner state of being and level of consciousness.

And right on time, there comes a cosmic mirror, to beam back this truth to us, in the shape of 2003 UB 313, better known as Dwarf Planet Eris.

Eris is presently some 98 astronomical units out from the Sun, approximately three times further out than Pluto, but according to astronomers her orbit will come in as close as Pluto's during her 557 year orbital path. She is presently moving through the Kuiper Belt furthest away from the Sun and as such is moving extremely slowly.

Since 1926 Eris has been in the Tropical Zodiacal sign of Aries, as seen from Earth, and will remain there until 2046, which means that the vast proportion of us, at the present time and all of us in a few years time, no matter which country, race or creed we come from, have, as a unifying focus and reflective mirror - Eris in Aries.

Right now, every man woman and 'child' under the age of 83 is held within this Eris in Aries archetypal resonance.

Sedna does indeed have a far longer orbital period, around 10,500 years, but because her orbit is so elliptical and at present she is close to Earth, at perihelion, during this same 120 year period, from 1926 to 2046, she will have passed through the Tropical zodiacal signs of Aries and Taurus and will have entered into Cancer.

So what is the archetypal resonance surrounding Eris? For those who do not know the mythology, here is a brief synopsis.

It is said that the Greek Goddess Eris was the personification of discord and strife, having the potential to stir up argument and disharmony. Certainly, Eris, according to tradition, has the potential to throw a spanner, or golden apple into the works and the family lineage does little to assuage the image of discord, for Eris's Mother, Nyx (Night) was born at the same time as Erebus (Primordial Darkness) out of Chaos and her sister, Ares, is said to be the Nurse of War.

Eris herself is best known for the part she played in the Trojan Wars. We are told that Eris was not invited by Zeus to a wedding that was to take place between Peleus and Thetis, the parents of Achilles, because of her reputation as a trouble maker. Eris angered by this exclusion decided to attend, and on the day of the wedding she stood outside the banquet room, rolled a Golden Apple, she had engraved with the words 'For the Fairest' across the floor and then left.

Aphrodite, the Goddess of Love and Beauty, Athena, the Goddess of Wisdom and Hera, the Goddess of the Olympians, all 'A' rated wedding guests, on seeing the apple began to argue who merited this title.

Zeus seeing that a fight was breaking out and not wanting to become involved, or to upset any of the Goddesses, decided to invite Paris of Troy to act as an arbitrator.

According to myth, all three Goddesses tried to bribe Paris - Athena offered him victory in battle, Hera offered him great wealth, and Aphrodite offered him the most beautiful woman on Earth – Helen of Troy.

Paris was swayed by Aphrodite's 'gift' and so gave to her the Golden Apple and title 'To the Fairest'. He sailed to Sparta and claimed Helen for himself.

There was just one small problem with this arrangement in that Helen was married to Menelaus at the time and when he found out that Helen had set sail for Troy with Paris as her lover, he and his brother, Agemennon, declared war against Troy and so began the chaos, pain and bloodshed of the Trojan Wars.

So now at the beginning of the 21st Century, as we enter into the Kuiper Belt and when Eris is back in our consciousness, what can we learn, understand and gain from this archetypal memory, myth and message that will help us at this present time?

One of the themes contained within the myth is how apparently unconnected trivial thoughts and actions can snowball into major events which can profoundly effect the lives of others.

Another of the messages is that our ego's competitive desire to be the best or 'Fairest' can wreak havoc. This deep insecurity underpins the story.

So the central message seems to be, that if we are to integrate the resonance of the planetary bodies within the Kuiper Belt, so as to access Galactic Consciousness, we need to have moved beyond the mind's desire to judge and compare – all coming from a deep vulnerability and sense of limitation and separation.

It is all too easy to point the finger at Eris, the Goddess of strife, for rolling the apple and for encouraging division, but each player has to own their own part in the drama that unfolds.

Looking at this drama without judgment one could say that the Goddesses could just as easily have picked the apple up and put it on the sideboard, but the decision taken by the three Goddesses to argue, clearly shows how insecurity, pride and vanity are powerful antidotes to love, beauty and wisdom.

This same lack of inner scrutiny is revealed within Zeus, who initially chose to judge Eris as unfit to attend the wedding. He then chose to sidestep defusing the argument between the Goddesses preferring to pass the buck to Paris who was a young shepherd and one who in his youth was apparently easily bribed by the thought of such a beautiful prize.

It is so much easier for all of the 'players' to ignore their actions and to point the finger of 'blame' at Eris.

Joseph Campbell who spoke so eloquently about the hero's journey and mythology in general said 'Your life is the fruit of your own doing. You have no one to blame but yourself.'

Blame is another facet of this story. For when blame and discord are set in motion, trivial action starts to snowball. Blame is such an unforgiving word, it speaks of pain and judgement that have congealed without resolution. How wonderful if 'blame' could vanish from our hearts and vocabulary in the 21st Century and be replaced with a deeply compassionate understanding that each of us has a 'mote' that we need to remove from our own eye if we are to look at the world with fresh, clear awareness.

For as a species, we have developed an instinctive reaction to pass on 'blame' to whoever will catch it.

Rather like a hot cinder, when things go apparently wrong, we look to see who we can throw the blame at before we burn our own fingers.

Discord and blame have been rolling around the Earth between individuals, races and religions for eons of time creating, division, strife and wars. With Eris, presently in Aries it is a perfect time for us each to face our shadows, our competitive streak, our mental judgments our warring tendencies, our sense of separation from self and others, and our unique ability to off load blame, which, if left to run unfettered, will continue to create such disharmony, division, chaos and pain.

As we are all passing through this resonance of Eris in Aries, we are each being handed a cosmic 'Golden Apple'. For Eris is informing and monitoring our individual and group level of consciousness as it responds to the ancestral karma that we have inherited at this point in time.

Are we going to continue to react and repeat disharmony, chaos and acts of war because of the past, or will we evolve and enter into a Galactic consciousness? This would seem to be the kernel of the question that is hidden within the story of Eris.

If we are to understand the message contained within this story, we need to see how Eris is asking us to go beyond the mental constructs of how we 'perceive' life simply through a dualistic mind, of good and bad, right and wrong, to a deep core 'knowing' that comes from the Soul.

For the Soul has the capacity to unify and harmonise, healing division and discord, heralding a profound shift of consciousness which ushers in the perfected seed - a unified family of Humane Beings.

Chapter 12

Collective Choice

'Mysterious coincidences cause the reconsideration of the inherent mystery that surrounds our individual lives on this planet.'

James Redfield *Author*

The coincidences and synchronicities surrounding Eris's orbital journey through the Tropical Zodiac ask that we become more aware of this distant messenger, for it is time to turn the cog of another spiral, to begin a fresh cycle, one that is no longer focussed on blame and attack.

If we go back, for a moment in time and look to see where Eris was, in the sky, around 9th September 2001, you will find that the months leading up to this moment in time, Eris was at 20 degrees of Aries – then a few days before 9/11 Eris moved back to the latter part of 19 degrees Aries.

In Dane Rudhyar's 'Astrological Mandala' 20 degrees of Aries has the image of 'A pugilist enters the ring' The theme for this degree is 'The release and glorification of social aggressiveness', the keynote being 'Overwhelming Power'

On the actual day Eris stood at 19 Aries which has as its image 'A young girl feeding birds in the winter' and has as its theme 'Overcoming crisis through compassion'.

The key for this degree is 'The transmutation of Life into Love'.

Certainly, the events of 9/11 would have required an immense transmutation of the collective consciousness to hold and heal the shock, fear, anger, and pain that flowed out across the airwaves on that September morning. However, the potential was there, in that moment in time, for compassion and wisdom to halt the flow of future karmic tidal waves, if the group consciousness, across the board, or holographic field, had so decreed.

This fundamental struggle of group consciousness continued to play out throughout the next years, as Eris moved backwards and forwards over 19 and 20 degrees of Aries.

Until, in June 2005, Eris moved briefly into 21 Aries which mirrors the image of 'The Gate to the Garden of all Fulfilled Desires' having as its theme 'Abundance made possible by human togetherness and co-operation'. The keynote for which is 'Cosmic optimism'

Eris, visits 20 Aries for the last time, in this cycle, during December 2009 to February 2010. It is a sensitive point that has been reflected back to us over the last eight years in the cyclic rise of terrorism and escalating violence in Iraq, Afghanistan and the Middle East.

Looking at the Table on the opposite page you can see how these two very different themes of 'The release and glorification of social aggressiveness' and 'Abundance made possible by human togetherness and co-operation' have been playing out through the collective during the last few years.

Eris Mirroring Collective Unconsciousness

06.2001	20 Aries	11.2007	20 Aries
09.2001	19 Aries	03.2008	21 Aries
05.2002	20 Aries	11.2008	20 Aries
10.2002	19 Aries	02.2009	21 Aries
04.2003	20 Aries	12.2009	20 Aries
11.2003	19 Aries	02.2010	21 Aries
03.2004	20 Aries	05.2010	22 Aries
11.2004	19 Aries	09.2010	21 Aries
03.2005	20 Aries	05.2011	22 Aries
06.2005	21 Aries	11.2011	21 Aries
08.2005	20 Aries	03.2012	22 Aries
01.2006	19 Aries	12.2012	21 Aries
01.2006	20 Aries	03.2013	22 Aries
05.2006	21 Aries	12.2013	21 Aries
09.2006	20 Aries	02.2014	22 Aries
04.2007	21 Aries	06.2014	23 Aries

From so many different Cosmic quarters we are being encouraged to take a giant step in our evolution, to walk away from conflict and aggression, finally recognising the karmic cycle and consequences that underpins and continuously circles within the psychic whole, until we as a group, consciously choose to call a halt to this madness and learn to live together.

If we truly embody and personify the essence and resonance of peace and 'Cosmic Optimism' within our minds and hearts and subconscious then, as a species, we have the real potential to see these gifts being reflected back to us across the Earth.

Back in the 1970's Joseph Conrad Pearce wrote 'The Crack in the Cosmic Egg' the focus of which was on what is perhaps the most difficult task facing us all as a human family – which is to surpass the traumatic conditioning of history and to enter upon a path of learning and healing, which truly reflects the potential of our species.

Quantum physics teaches us that we are each connected within a holographic field, that our individual essences affect the whole grid and so each of us has the potential, through our heightened resonance, to bring about a shift of consciousness to our history of fighting and pain.

All spiritual traditions speak of compassion as the pathway to enlightenment. For the last 2000 years or so, as Pisces has been the silent, stellar backdrop through which we have all been experiencing our lives, we have had the opportunity to leave behind our basic fears and to evolve into an intelligent compassionate and evolved species.

The resonance of Neptune, the planetary ruler of Pisces, whose journey through the Cosmos distributes a pure resonance and essence out through the Solar System, which has been flowing through us all, like Manna from Heaven, as we walk upon this Earth.

Neptune has the potential to expand us into other worlds, other states, softly peeling away resistance, gently guiding us towards greater sensitivity, refined feeling, compassion - helping us all on our journey to becoming humane beings centred in our hearts.

It was on the 24th of September 1846, in Berlin, that Neptune was 'discovered' and since then we have all had the opportunity to connect to this transcendent energy consciously.

As I am completing this book, Neptune is about to complete the first orbital journey around the Sun, on 11th April 2009, once more returning to its discovery point in space at 25 Aquarius 52.

In the Discovery Chart of 1846, Neptune was conjunct Saturn, both retrograde, on this degree, 150 degrees away from Mars, which in turn, was 150 degrees away from the South Nodal point conjunct, a yet to be discovered Pluto, forming a Yod.

The Discovery Chart speaks of transformation and growth that is possible through the energetics of the Yod that is formed.

Mars is the focal point of this Yod, or Finger of God, focusing and emphasising the need to harness personal, individualistic drive and competition via the temperance of Saturn and Neptune so as to create a more collective sense of purpose and in so doing, transform the misuse of collective and personal power within the South Nodal point conjunct Pluto in Aries.

Pluto in Aries and Mars as the focal point of this Yod is a powerful reflective mirror to see how we will, as a group consciousness learn to harness these forces and transform them to higher potential.

Pluto is the gateway into Galactic Consciousness, the doorway into an awareness of a life beyond the wars and battles of human dramas and power struggles.

There is a real sense of a need for temperance and, indeed of personal sacrifice in order to grow beyond reactive aggression, which is reflected in the natal Sun position which is at 0 Libra 31.

Referring once again to 'An Astrological Mandala', this degree has as its image, 'In a collection of perfect specimens of many biological forms, a butterfly displays the beauty of its wings, its body impaled by a fine dart.'

Dane Rudhyar speaks of this image reflecting 'A perfect form' The metamorphosis of a worm into a butterfly... the trans-human being, the true Initiate.... the Son of Man 'impaled by Divine Light making of him a Son of God. The human individual made sacred.'

A yet to be discovered Chiron in Libra opposes Uranus in Aries, again giving a real sense of how we may be wounded if we do not learn to harness our unfettered and ill considered acts of wilful personal and collective actions.

Chiron opposite Uranus seems to offer us, once again, the fire of Prometheus, the spark of Divine Light, that Dane Rudhyar speaks of that ignites our minds and hearts with passion to reach beyond the current awareness of that time. To grow beyond the limitations of collective belief takes courage and strength, but both are available within this moment in time with Mars at the focal point of the Yod.

A profoundly transformational journey was being offered through the unfolding of this moment in time during the first conscious cycle of Neptune.

Having now completed the first cycle of Neptune around the Sun, since it was discovered in 1846, we know that, as a group, we have witnessed many wars and battles during this period.

Was this the necessary wounding that Rudhyar referred to, in order for us to focus our consciousness on radical change.

Have we now all had enough of this destructive madness?

To see how the next cycle of Neptune around the Sun has the potential to unfold let us look at Neptune's Return Chart of April 2009. You will see that Neptune has once again returned to 25 Aquarius 52, but this time, instead of Saturn being conjunct, in perfect timing, Chiron, steps in to accompany Neptune at the start of this cycle.

These two planets form a stellium with Jupiter in Aquarius. Chiron's connection to any planetary body, intensifies, refines, and spiritualizes the resonance of that planetary vibration, as Chiron's resonance has the potential to increase the light quotient in physical cellular matter.

A stellium of Jupiter, Neptune and Chiron in Aquarius is the personification of Universal Love which seeks to manifest through this next cycle.

In this Return Chart the Sun is at 21 Aries sextile to Jupiter, Chiron and Neptune. 21 Aries, if you remember, was also the orbital position of Eris in April 2009.

Is this just a coincidence or perfect symmetry and Divine timing?

Interpreting this Return chart we can see that in order to unfold the highest potential of Jupiter, Chiron and Neptune through our consciousness, we will need to have truly worked through the messages contained within the archetype of Eris if we are, indeed, to step into the 'The Gate to the Garden of all Fulfilled Desires' and to 'Abundance made possible by human togetherness and co-operation'.

Out in the dark space of the Kuiper Belt Eris is acting as a reflective mirror to our toxicity, encouraging, cajoling and focussing us all on the opportunity that we have to break free from past history and to come together as a humane family in space, a unique and precious group who presently reside on the outer limits of the Heart of the Galaxy.

In leaving behind our fearful, aggressive, survival tactics, honed over centuries and centuries, we step closer to the Light at the centre of our Galaxy and to the influx of spiritual energy.

Once again Eris is the mirror that reflects this potential back to us for, in mid June 2014, she will enter 23 Aries where, all us will be bathed in the image that shimmers down through the Cosmos offering 'An Openness to the Influx of Spiritual Energies', where 'The Mind is Moulded by Transpersonal Force'.

You may think that this is pure coincidence, just an overactive imagination at work, but I prefer to think like the philosopher, Frederich Schiller, that 'There is no such thing as chance; and what seems to us merest accident springs from the deepest source of Destiny.'

As a species we are at this moment of Destiny.

Neptune Discovery Chart

24th September 1846
Berlin

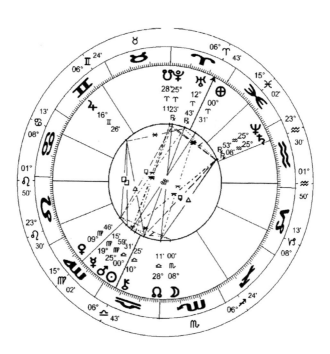

Neptune Return Chart

11 April 2009
8.30 CEDT
Berlin Germany

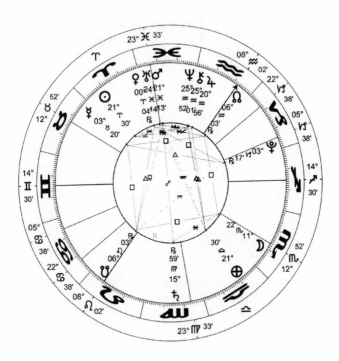

Chapter 13

Destiny Calls

Imagine all the people living life in peace...
You may say that I'm a dreamer but I'm not the only one
I hope someday you'll join us and the world will be as one

John Lennon *Musician*

So what is destiny? It is thought to be the fixed order of things; invincible necessity; fate; a resistless power or agency conceived of as determining the future; a condition foreordained by the Divine for both the individual and collective.

From this perspective it appears that we are powerless before the hands of Destiny. Destiny would seem to weave an invisible membrane through our lives, in which events unfold which have an immovable predestination.

Another, perhaps more accurate, description of destiny might be a moment in time when a choice is made coming from the collective group consciousness.

As astrologers, our ability to see the potential unfolding of future events links to this sense of predestination. It is a great gift to be an astrologer. All of us will remember our first steps into this Hall of Knowledge, Like iron filings, all of us were drawn to come to study and love the symmetry, geometry and pure magic of a mystery unfolding before our eyes.

As astrologers, we can play an integral part in the evolutionary process, as we have the larger canvas on which to watch our unfolding consciousness and we have our fingers on the Cosmic pulse, as such we can see the colour of the litmus paper for any given moment in time.

We can watch how the individual or group respond to these moments in time. In the past we may have seen the response as something outside of ourselves rather than a true reflection of our inner being, our unconscious creations.

Carl Jung believed that the uncovering, or bringing to light, of the unconsciousness was the greatest spiritual task that mankind could undertake,

This journey to clarity, to mastery of self, is the pathway to our evolution beyond our confined thinking and belief that we are in some way inevitably fated.

When we look at planetary patterns we can see only potential, for there are a multitude of possibilities that can flow from any combination of planetary aspects, the manifestation of which reflects the consciousness and the resonance of the individual and the collective environmental field.

We, as astrologers, of all souls on the planet, have the ability to witness and understand the health of the individual and collective psyche through the physical manifestations of 'destiny' that occur at certain moments in time. That is what we do as astrologers.

However, rather like voyeurs we often dissect a chart to reveal what planetary patterns were occurring that 'created' a particular situation rather than addressing and recognising our collective and individual central role in any creation that occurs on planet Earth.

Over the next decades, as science and mysticism inevitably draw closer together as more is revealed and discovered, astrology does have the potential to become a central pillar in our understanding of how we are intimately interconnected, through our consciousness, with each other, the Earth and the wider Cosmos.

But we have to step away from any sense that stars and planets are solely responsible for our 'fate' this very thought both negates our self responsibility and our own creative potential.

In the past, prior to our knowledge of any interconnecting holographic field, it might have appeared as if planets and stars, solely dictated an outcome in some arbitrary manner in which we were not personally involved.

However, we now know that the Cosmos is resonating within the subtle energetic field and there is a profound and direct two way communication occurring that is reflecting our individual levels of consciousness.

It is true to say that each of the planets through their mass, density and orbital speed, set up an individual resonance that we interpret within our physical frame, however, our response to these planetary cycles is coloured through our own receptive vehicle.

In *The Biology of Belief* Bruce Lipton describes how each of our cells has a surrounding membrane. This membrane is highly responsive to the environmental field that encompasses it. Each membrane has a vast array of proteins which receive and transmit information, maintaining the health or otherwise of the cell, from the environmental field.

As astrologers, we are able to understand, that our subtle environmental field stretches way beyond our immediate surroundings, out into the Solar System, Galaxy and beyond and our interactive response to this living, conscious field is reflected via our thoughts, feelings and actions, which in turn is reflected within the health and wellbeing of each membrane surrounding each cell within our body.

This incredible interchange of information is not handled by our surface mind – but is handled by our deepest levels of unconsciousness. Each cell has an intelligence and a direct link not only to each other cell but out to Source.

In this microscopic world, housed within our physical form, universes are reflected at play. For in just the same way as we are composed of billions of cells, so too is the Galaxy composed of billions of stars and planets and our Earth is just one cell within this vast system.

From this vantage point, one cell in our human body is a mirror image of the Earth flowing in, another body, the Galaxy.

Bruce Lipton likens human beings to the proteins found on an individual cell, in that we are the receivers and transmitters of information.

Like the proteins on each individual cell, we, through our connection to the Earth and the Cosmos, are the conduits through which balance and evolutionary growth occurs within the 'cell' of Earth, within our own beings, and then back out into the environmental field of the Universe.

In maintaining the health of our own cellular system, like the proteins on individual cells, we are intimately maintaining the wellbeing of our precious, life giving home – Mother Earth.

When the American astronaut Edgar Mitchell looked out into space, in one heart stopping moment he saw the Earth with fresh eyes and said - 'Suddenly, from behind the rim of the Moon, in long, slow-motion moments of immense majesty, there emerges a sparkling blue and white jewel, a light, delicate sky-blue sphere laced with slowly swirling veils of white, rising gradually like a small pearl in a thick sea of black mystery. It takes more than a moment to fully realize this is Earth . . . home. My view of our planet was a glimpse of Divinity.'

On another journey out into space, but with the same epiphany of awareness, the Russian astronaut Aleksei Leonov said: 'The Earth was small, light blue, and so touchingly alone - our home that must be defended like a holy relic. The Earth was absolutely round. I believe I never knew what the word round meant until I saw Earth from space.'

Seeing the Earth as a single round cell within the vastness of space, we too, just like the astronauts, can come to see just how we assist, or detract from the environmental field that we live within.

We can come to see how interdependent we are upon each other, how each thought and feeling flows out into the whole that we share.

Just as we each breathe from the same shared reservoir of air, so too we will come to recognise, do we share the mental and emotional environment that we inhabit on Mother Earth.

We will also come to realise that Life, in truth, is a magical, sacred experience - a dance in time and all of us have the potential to consciously participate at the Ball. Each of us is intimately connected to the well being of our Planet.

As we move into this Age of Aquarius our shared humanity is reflected in the, peace, health and well being of our home in space. How relevant then, that the last Dwarf Planet to be given 'status' in our recently realigned Solar System, is Ceres, for Ceres is the Goddess and the Guardian of crops.

Again, is it coincidence that at this period of our history, there are crop circles appearing around the world. The greatest focus of these crop circles have manifested down in Wiltshire, England close to Avebury and Silbury Hill, ancient monuments that have stood on the land for thousands of years.

First appearing in the early 1980's, they have been coming thick and fast ever since – beautiful in their intricacy and inexplicable in their presence. When seen from the air they are breathtaking in their precision, mathematical elegance and sheer mind blowing wonder.

There are many theories as to how these crop circles manifest, but, however they are occurring, we need to recognise that nature and this Universe is abundantly powerful and capable of much beyond our present awareness.

When things are inexplicable there is a tendency to dismiss them – but we need to look more closely at what is appearing down in those quiet Wiltshire fields, for we are witnessing a phenomena which is breaking the patterns of our current knowledge.

Aerial View of Two 2009 Crop Circles

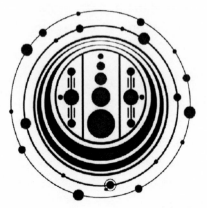

Adam Beamish 2009

Tommy Borms 2009

We are being taken into a much larger field.

As the protector of the harvest, or the crops, Ceres is intimately interconnected to the heart and health of the planet whose wellbeing is reflected within the abundance of golden harvests.

Rather than feeling overwhelmed at this point in time with so many changes and inexplicable happenings occurring, we need to know that we can play a pivotal part in the birthing of this new field of consciousness.

Imagine, how wonderful it would be to embody the image of Earth as a golden field, of pure light, bursting with life, health and well being.

Imagine each cell or your body reflecting this same pure energetic field.

Imagine how wonderful if would be to live consciously creating well being, for all, sowing the seeds that unite all nations creeds and beliefs into one loving, humane family which nurtures and protects all life forms on this planet.

Is this just dreaming, or a true potential?

Within this holographic field that supports all life we are co-creating our realities within the Cosmic field.

The cycles of the planets that flow through this immense Life Force are there to assist us to evolve beyond our human frailties and differing ideologies.

The Cosmos has no racial, gender or religious bias the cycles of the planets simply reflect the consciousness of the individual for we are all held within a pure, loving, sustaining, Cosmic Field that births creation.

As astrologers we have watched this apparent, moving hand of destiny unfold across time, both in the collective and in the individual and now it is time for us all to begin the process of healing the divisions and arguments that have rolled around our planet for so long.

If we are to act as guides and way showers within this unfolding cosmic field then we need to have walked a few footsteps ahead, so that we may open the minds and hearts of those we encounter to the expansion of consciousness and potential that surrounds us and is our inheritance.

As we begin to truly explore our inner universe that is revealed within the microcosm of cellular activity and reconnect to the ancient wisdom that recognises that we are all creators, within a divine field of consciousness, we will step into a whole new level of evolutionary awareness. We will truly come to know that we are not separate from the Universe, but are truly a physical manifestation of this loving consciousness.

We are at this moment of destiny, but this destiny requires that we too consciously participate in this unfolding cycle of time.

All of us are involved in this quantum shift of consciousness and just like the visionary Richard Buckminster Fuller, said 'On space ship Earth there are no passengers – everyone is crew'.

As part of the crew, we can light the way for others as we journey onward.

For we are the messengers of the unfolding Cosmos and we are the torch bearers of the future wishing to manifest, so let us spread the message far and wide, across the land and out across the Universe as we, once again, remember our true purpose and potential.

Lightning Source UK Ltd.
Milton Keynes UK
16 December 2009

147611UK00001B/1/P